Laila

Held for a Moment

A MEMOIR

Versions of this story appeared as follows:
*Chapter Ten appeared in *Barren Magazine*
*Chapter Eleven appeared in *Macro Magazine*

*This book is based on real events though names of
certain places and people have been changed in order
to protect the privacy of individuals.*

Cover design by Michelle Fairbanks, Fresh Design
Interior formatting by Amanda Reid for Melissa Williams Design
Prepared for Publication by Write | Publish | Sell

ISBN (paperback): 9781955119337
Library of Congress Control Number: 2022903563

Printed in the United States of America

Laila

Held for a Moment

A MEMOIR

Leah Mele-Bazaz

KAT BIGGIE PRESS

To Laila

PREFACE

The Great American Eclipse arrived for the first time in a hundred years. Like others, curiosity nudged me to step out of the office to witness the commotion. The full moon blotted out the afternoon sun like a shaded bubble in a standardized test. For a few moments, the city hid in total darkness. Days later, I found out I was expecting my daughter.

After she died, the darkness returned, and the sun seemed to disappear for months, even years. For a while, silence suffocated me. At a young age, I had learned from my great-grandmother Hilda's experience that children shouldn't die, and if they do, it's kept in the dark.

Hilda had a daughter, Diane, that no one ever spoke about. Diane suffered a brain injury as an infant from a collapsed crib, and never was the same after. Growing up, Diane often tried to escape her home into busy streets until my great-grandfather learned of a place to send her.

Diane had been institutionalized. I imagined Hilda's hands shaking in the passenger seat as she prayed the Rosary in her mind, pleading silently with God for her girl to be safe while my great-grandfather drove them to the state facility. Hilda often visited, telling her other daughter, my grandmother, that the living conditions were horrible; the children looked like they were kept in cages.

I had only overheard bits and pieces about Diane and why she had never returned. *She escaped her room one day and was found outside, eating grass.* I imagined her running down the narrow, winding halls, fleeing through the doors, splaying herself on a patch of the vast grounds of the asylum in her long white gown as the rain poured down on her. She swallowed handfuls and died shortly after at the age of sixteen.

Hilda never learned the cause of death. What if her daughter had died from one of those terrible procedures? What if someone had hurt her? I wondered if Hilda had tried to find the records of her daughter at the state asylum, if she had conducted an autopsy of her daughter, like I had for Laila.

Over the years, I watched my great-grandmother grieve in silence. No one ever mentioned that daughter. You could sometimes hear Hilda calling out for her in her sleep, "My sweet girl, Diane."

Hilda visited the grave each year on the girl's birthday, looming over her headstone as she leaned on her marble-colored cane. Her daughter's plot was in between hers and her husband's. "I'll be next to my baby and husband soon," she'd tell me as I clasped her soft, veiny hand.

She had cloudy blue eyes and smelled of lavender and Pond's cream. A patterned scarf covered her pure-white hair, which she always kept pinned back with bobby pins. Although Hilda lived one hundred and one years, I never dared to ask her about her daughter's death; I knew it had caused estrangement within the family.

Grievers often talk about the blurred line between life and death after a loved one dies. Some see signs from their loved ones from beyond, like a red robin visiting their doorstep. Hilda had been born with a "veil" over her head, known as an en caul birth, emerging from the birth canal while still tucked inside the translucent amniotic sac. In Norway, where her mother was from, our ancestors believed this extremely rare occurrence meant she was gifted with second sight. Sailors would even bring the baby's caul with them to prevent their ships from sinking.

Hilda was clairvoyant, a trait passed down my maternal line. She could sense who was calling her before caller ID was invented. She also saw things. The day her brother tragically died in a car accident, she was sitting in her living room when a white apparition flashed across the window, so intense that even my grandmother saw it. "That's my brother," she said in a hollow voice. When my great-grandmother saw things like that, it was taken as fact.

Like my great-grandmother, I've often experienced moments of intuition and have seen otherworldly, haunting things. It started with visions at night. I would wake up screaming from the sight of a woman at the foot of my bed, or a man without a head walking around in boxers. I'd call for my mother, and she would give me orange juice out of my pink sippy cup to lull me back to sleep. The pediatrician called them *night terrors* and said I would outgrow them, but I never did.

I have often experienced this gift of second sight with my daughter, seeing and hearing things I was afraid to recognize. Perhaps, all along, I knew my baby would die and there was nothing I could do, no matter how hard I tried. This story is my caul, and I hang it here in hopes of preventing other sailors' ships from sinking.

CHAPTER ONE

You're pregnant. I tried to shake the small whisper I kept hearing over and over again. A few weeks ago, a small voice had said, *You just conceived,* after I spent the night with my boyfriend, Gautam. I was on the pill and doubted that had really happened, but later I felt the possibility of a pregnancy with such intensity that I found myself at the pharmacy on my lunch break.

Tugging my light cardigan around my shoulders, I scanned the aisles until I found the family planning section, categorized under "Feminine Health." *Go figure.* As I passed the hygiene products and cranberry pills, the sneaking suspicion that I was pregnant grew on me. The tests were shelved next to the lube and condoms, and even the cheapest one was sealed in a glass case that would require an employee to unlock it. I pressed my finger on the buzzer to get the attention of the staff. A loud beeping emanated from the speaker, making blood rush to my face. When the employee handed me the box, I avoided eye contact and rushed to the counter.

As I paid the twenty bucks for the pregnancy

test, I still wasn't sure why I was bothering to buy one, let alone in the middle of a workday. My period was supposed to arrive soon, but that inner voice had been growing louder all day. Work was a little slow, and I had to know, so I jammed the cardboard box into my shoulder bag and hurried back to my office.

As a recent college graduate, it was unusual that I had my own office at the finance firm. The stuffy yellow-carpeted office was hardly larger than a closet, piled with recording equipment for the financial podcast I helped produce. But still, it was a room of my own. Its noise-canceling oak doors and lack of windows provided me privacy from the men in the bullpen when I needed it. I'd done my best to make it mine, adding a circular, embroidered carpet that Gautam had bought me during his last trip to Delhi.

The moment I walked in, I spotted a stack of blazers lying over the back of my chair that I hadn't gotten around to taking to the dry cleaners. After hanging them on the hook behind the door, I slid off my work mules beneath the desk, took a seat, and got to work.

The possibility of motherhood swirled around my mind like a milky cappuccino. If I were pregnant, Gautam would be a good dad. I'd witnessed how good he was with his young nephews. We had been together for a year, and that was notable. My relationships usually had a shelf life like a carton of milk: Sweet at first, but they'd sour fast. Gautam was different, maybe because he was thirteen years older than me and more mature.

On our first date, I didn't scare him away. I had recently completed Reiki training with a spiritualist, and all I could talk about was spirituality and the beyond. The training had heightened my abilities to see otherworldly things. I rambled on about how I had communicated with a good friend's deceased aunt and how she'd told me about a family heirloom tucked away in her jewelry box.

"Do you believe in ghosts?" I asked him as I sipped on my ruby slipper cocktail, a heavenly mix of white wine, champagne, and cherries. Typical with any first date, I needed a drink to relax.

"My grandfather actually could see things like you," he said with a smirk. "Once, after work at his government job in India, he walked out of the building and ran into a man in a stagecoach pulled by a black horse. The coachman warned him to take the other way home and not to pass over the bridge. Only later did my grandfather learn that the same man had died when the bridge had collapsed only hours before."

"That's spooky as hell," I said as I ate a cheese cube and swallowed my drink. The restaurant, designed like a speakeasy, was very dark, with small candles providing the only light, and Gautam's complexion was tan and warm in the dim glow. He was too attractive to be my type—I thought that if I wasn't attracted to the man I dated, I wouldn't be as likely to get hurt. I'd spent my early twenties goofing off with men, repeating toxic cycles like it was my part-time job. Healthy relationships bored me, and I'd lose interest.

"Do you think you'd ever be a medium?" he asked as he sipped on a beer.

"Oh, God, no," I said.

In all honesty, my spirituality was a headache. I had only signed up for Reiki training after my physical therapist had suggested it to more holistically manage chronic neck pain from a car accident, not to enhance my second sight. My abilities were more burdensome than helpful. Presences wanting to communicate frequently kept me up at night, and I often had to bathe in essential oils and salt to keep the spirits away. When my training was complete, it was a relief.

We went home together that night. He wanted to take things slow, but I insisted on moving fast. Things were different with him, and I didn't feel nervous. Our hands were all over each other. Sweat dripped off our bodies onto the duvet. Pillows sprawled across the queen-sized mattress were used as props for better positions to get closer. My hands clenched the corner of the bed, pulling back the fitted sheet and exposing the bare mattress by the end of it. I felt safe around him.

While the sex was good, love scared me. I often attempted to push his love away, but he was like a springboard. I wasn't used to this, and I caught myself falling for him. I never pictured myself married, but his resilience made me think he was the right sort of man to have a baby with. If he could keep someone like me in a relationship, he could hold a family together.

I tried to draft an email, but I found myself

staring at the blinking cursor. Men in the small kitchenette refilled stale coffee that had been in the pot since the morning. The microwave chimed. Dishes clanked. I closed my office doors. Maybe all these pregnancy thoughts were due to a runaway imagination—either way, I needed to know. I slipped my mules back on and grabbed my bag and went into the bathroom. It wasn't easy working in a male-dominated office, but one perk was that I almost always had the ladies' room completely to myself.

I took the box from my purse and pulled out the test. Without hesitation, I slid up my dress, yanked down my underwear, and hovered over the porcelain toilet bowl. *What a sight*, I thought as I held the flimsy pregnancy test between my legs. With my other hand, I yanked free a piece of paper towel and laid the test out on the counter. Then I waited for my urine to provide the verdict. Lo and behold, my intuition was right. Two pink lines appeared on the plastic applicator.

I could hardly believe it. Adrenaline rushed through my body, reminding me of how I used to feel at the start of a cross-country race. Before the starting pistol went off, my pulse would get so loud that all other sounds would fade.

That little voice in my head had been right. Weird. Even weirder, I had assumed an unexpected pregnancy would be scary. While I trembled at the daunting idea of motherhood, it felt like a secret door had been unlocked, and I was hungry for it. I simply hadn't realized how much I wanted a baby, *this baby*, until that moment.

The few blocks of Philadelphia's financial district encompassed a couple of skyscrapers, nothing like its more charming neighbor New York. By mere coincidence or fate, Gautam and I worked in the same crimson red tower, him at a healthcare start-up and me at a private wealth management firm. We'd agreed to meet downstairs on the patio after work.

Despite being full of working adults, the outdoor terrace resembled a high school lunchroom. The smokers hung out in the corner, construction workers gathered on a bench with their sandwiches, and the occasional office worker drank a fresh-pressed smoothie. Older people shuffled to the nearby train to get back to the suburbs, while younger ones lined up outside the building to access the rooftop happy hour.

I made my way to an empty table near the fountain, where the sound of rushing water soothed me. It had rained the night before, so I grabbed some napkins out of my purse to dry the seats off. As I did, I noticed the wrapped pregnancy test, which I had decided to keep as a souvenir.

Gautam seemed to move in slow motion as he stepped through the rotating doors and walked over to me. He was too well dressed for Philly in his Canali suit, which complemented his broad shoulders.

He sat down so fast that I didn't even have time to warn him. He'd taken the one chair I hadn't dried off. As a child, his family had called him Go-Go; he had always been moving and rushing about.

"Are you okay?" he asked, unphased by the wet seat. Maybe it wasn't as bad as I thought.

I scrunched my nose in response, something I did when I was nervous. My throat felt tight.

"I think I'm pregnant," I said in a soft voice, careful not to let anyone overhear. We hadn't been trying, but we did have a lot of sex.

"Really?" His brow furrowed over his round eyes. I couldn't tell if he was terrified or happy.

"I took a test," I said, feeling self-conscious. It was very strange to have taken the pregnancy test at work, I realized.

"We can make this work," he said and gently placed his hand on mine. The initial shock left his face, replaced by a smile.

"I know we can." I grasped his hands, thrilled that he was on board. Even if he hadn't been, I would have made it work. I felt connected to this child like a magnet had been placed inside my belly. But I was glad that we were doing this together.

"My pants are wet," he added.

"I tried to wipe that down for you," I said and laughed.

He playfully rolled his eyes and teased, "Uh-huh, sure you did." Then he hugged me, only to pull back for a moment. "What made you take a test?"

"I'm not sure. I had a feeling."

⊱✿⊰

After work, we took a walk. Gautam held my laptop bag for me as I wobbled through the city like I had sea legs. We passed through Center City and then wandered over the pedestrian bridge to West Philly. At the University of Pennsylvania, students lounged outside, watching a Disney movie, *Moana*, projected on a screen set up on the manicured lawn, an oasis in the surrounding city.

"We have some planning to do," Gautam said. He took comfort in logistics. It was easier for us to discuss action items than the daunting idea of parenthood. An animated chicken on the screen made the students cackle with laughter.

"Is that right?" I was impressed by his initiative as I smacked off a mosquito.

We claimed a bench behind the group of undergraduates. I was familiar with the campus, as I had studied Urdu here in high school. I loved the hiss of the words I'd learned, so different from English as they rolled off my tongue with passionate sounds like *hai*. On the last day of the summer language class, we'd filmed a skit about an Indian wedding as our final project; I'd played the bride.

Gautam put his arms around me and pulled me close. "Once we share the news with our family, we can plan a small wedding."

"How small is small?" I teased. As an introvert, a big wedding was unappealing to me. I knew that hundreds of relatives had attended his sister's traditional wedding. I didn't even like wedding dresses. As a young girl, my mother would share stories about how I'd thrown tantrums when I'd had to wear puffy dresses.

"I promise we'll keep the list down. Maybe we'll have a larger, traditional Indian ceremony after the baby. We'll make this as low-key as possible."

"That doesn't sound so bad," I said, annoyed at the flutters in my chest. Whatever hold-up I had about marriage and happily ever after, the walls I had built after failed relationships had crumbled down with him. With our baby on the way, all felt right in the world.

We hung back to watch the end of the movie, with Moana sailing across the sea to save her island. At the end of the credits, the production baby names flashed on the screen, and all the babies born during the making of the movie claimed their seconds of fame. I could picture the proud parents showing their kids this movie. Years later, I learned from another loss mom that *Moana* is the only Disney film with a star next to a baby's name who died during production.

To make sure that the results of the first pregnancy test weren't a mistake, we stopped at a pharmacy to get a digital one. This time around, I scooped up a bottle of prenatal vitamins and added it to the flimsy bag. Then we cut through Rittenhouse Square, a two-block historical park in Center City. Unlike the other city parks, like Washington Square, this one wasn't a former burial ground. In the summer, the fountain in the reflecting pool was full. Children liked to squeal and dip their feet in it. I imagined our future child doing the same.

Back at the apartment, I slid off my flats and noticed the new blisters on my heels from the walk. Gautam turned on the lights and made his way into the kitchen to grab me a glass of water. Before handing the drink to me, he paused to water the plant, Ernie, a dracaena. Ernie was a prized possession. When Gautam was a bachelor, Ernie had been the only other living thing in my husband's condo. Over the holidays, Ernie is our Charlie Brown Christmas tree, and we keep the white lights on him year-round. Whenever Gautam traveled for work, I was tasked with making sure Ernie had enough water. Once, when he had business in Dubai, I overwatered Ernie; I didn't realize dracaenas don't require much water.

Our home was small, but it was enough for just the two of us. He'd bought the condo nearly ten years ago after the market crash, and after our first date, he'd cleaned out a drawer for me to stash my belongings. I was amused by how we naturally fit together and wanted to be close. I had never lived with anyone before, not even in college. I'd always had a single dorm. Over the year of dating, I'd ended up with a closet to myself and a bathroom cabinet.

I chugged the glass of water and scanned our condo with a new set of eyes. It had everything we needed: a living room, a small nook for the dining table, and a large bedroom with Juliet balcony doors. Now, though, we'd have to make room for a baby. I wondered if the space worked or if we needed to move.

Gautam joined me in the bathroom as we waited for the second pregnancy test results. The digital monitor glowed YES. We laughed at how assertive and affirmative it was, and we kept saying, "YES, YES, YES."

I drew a lukewarm bath before bed. With wet fingers, I scrolled through my contact list, eager to tell someone else. I decided to message a friend from college, one of the few I'd stayed in touch with after transferring from a small liberal arts college to a university in the city. I had started shampooing my hair when she called me. After rubbing my hand against the towel, I answered.

"You know, there are always other options . . ." she said in a deeper tone, not her usual bubbly voice. "You're so young."

A sick feeling coiled in my belly like a snake. "No," I said as I sat upright in the tub. My hands began to shake. "I *want* my baby."

She paused. "Right. Shit. I'm sorry."

I was twenty-four, but I didn't feel so young. I felt ready to be a parent, but I didn't know how to show her. I hoped our families would be encouraging. I squeezed the body wash into my palm and scrubbed my legs, belly, and breasts until I was covered in a soapy lather. Then I submerged myself in the water until I was clean.

Chapter Two

I didn't have a primary care doctor. My last visit had been at my hometown pediatrician's office back in New Jersey, where the doctor very politely informed me that, at twenty-four, I was way too old to continue going there. "Soon enough, you'll have kids of your own," she'd told me. I'd laughed at that; the notion sounded ridiculous. As a parting gift, the receptionist handed me a lollipop-filled mug filled that declared: *Congrats! I graduated from my time here at the pediatrician's alive and well.* After my daughter died, I would drink from the chipped mug and find myself feeling sour over the assumption that all children live.

I booked an appointment at a local women's practice. I was self-conscious without a ring on my finger, so I put on my professional business clothes to look older for my first appointment. Instead of a basic office suite like in the suburbs, the practice was in an old, repurposed brownstone. I passed the office without realizing it and needed to backtrack. The tucked-away building blended in with the other walk-up apartments. In one of the small examination rooms, the doctor confirmed my pregnancy—and then asked if I'd like to keep my baby.

My confidence plummeted. I glanced down at my blazer, feeling like an idiot. I hadn't realized that this was a standard question that most women were asked during pregnancies. I assumed I looked young.

"Yes," I replied in a firm voice. I felt defensive, and I wanted to justify my decision to the doctor, to tell her that, although we weren't rich, we had enough to sustain another life. I had health insurance, I could easily make my student loan payments, I had a retirement plan, and I could start a 529 plan. I also had decent savings, since I'd lived at home until I'd met Gautam. His start-up business would take off eventually. It would be work, but we could do it.

"Great," she said with a bright smile. Then she calculated the due date for me: June 11, 2018.

A summer baby! That cheered me up. I'd always felt bad for classmates born in the summer, because they never got to share cupcakes or birthday wishes with other students during the school year. I was already thinking about ways to make a summer birthday fun. Our residential building had an outdoor pool, and I imagined birthday parties on the deck, with ice-cream cake and water ice, the Philly classic.

As I walked home, the doctor's words suddenly weighed on me: *Are you keeping your baby?* I arrived at the apartment with tears in my eyes. *Pregnancy hormones*, I thought.

"You'll be a great mom," Gautam said. "We'll

find a new doctor."

After a few unsuccessful visits to other facilities; Gautam's doctor friend referred us to Dr. C.

We had a consultation with her, and it was like love at first sight. She was wearing scrubs and a zip-up jacket with the hospital logo on it, and her short, soft curls were in a low bun. She seemed different from other doctors, who usually rushed from one appointment to the next. She was patient and gentle with our questions, and she treated me like the mother I longed to be.

CHAPTER THREE

One evening, the glow of Gautam's phone disrupted my sleep. I tugged the worn covers over my face and brushed him off, not wanting to wake—I prized sleep even more now that I was pregnant. With the balcony doors open in the bedroom, the last of the crisp fall weather circulated through the room.

"Just look," Gautam said as he pulled the brown comforter lower. The screen was back, shining through my eyelids.

"What is it?" I moaned.

"Here," he said in a quieter voice. When his voice got quiet, that meant he was upset. I opened my eyes.

"I'm sorry. Let me see." I squinted at the small screen. A graphic loaded of a plane ticket with my name written on it.

"Oh my God," I said as I brought his face to mine and kissed him. "Iceland!"

"For your birthday," he added, confirming my greatest hopes before kissing me again. In a few weeks, we were heading to Iceland. My one travel dream was to see the northern lights. During bad days in college, after I'd quit the cross-country team my sophomore year, I'd search online for images of the aurora borealis, promising myself that once I graduated, I would see the wonder for myself.

While I'd traveled to Mexico and Canada, my travel life remained "like NAFTA." In contrast, Gautam had traveled to more than sixty countries, but even he had never been to Iceland. This would be our first time together in a new country, and with the right weather conditions, in a few weeks, my dream of seeing the northern lights would come to pass.

Gautam knew that I didn't do well on longer flights, and he took that into consideration when planning the itinerary. After we landed, we checked in at a hostel by the airport to take a nap before our long drive south. When I woke, Gautam wanted to make sure I got some food. To settle my nausea, I peeled a salted hard-boiled egg and ate it in the communal kitchen.

Then we picked up our rental car and drove for hours through the countryside. Gautam had heard you're more likely to see the lights if you stay far from the city. The desolate landscape turned dark, lonely, and bleak, like a scene out of *Jane Eyre*.

On the way, we stopped at one of the country's many famous waterfalls, where I learned the Icelandic word for it: foss. I imagined the thunderous waterfall holding ancient secrets. We looked at the rushing water for so long, feeling its spray on our face, that we swore we saw shapes in the mist. I envisioned liminal beings folk dancing to the music of the booming water, their hands interlocked as they rejoiced.

Next, we passed a field of wild Icelandic ponies, and then we spotted a local museum. Inside, I read through pamphlets of the terrifying folklore of monsters who ate children and elves who stole babies.

"Does this creep you out?" I asked Gautam as we stared at a figurine of a fairy made from twigs, standing in a glass case.

"Not at all. Wait until you come to India. Monkeys snatch babies there, too," he teased as he grabbed my hips.

On our first night, we had no luck with the northern lights. We both dreamed about an Icelandic troll sneaking into our hotel room. In my dream, the hairy troll pried open the window and slipped into the room. In Gautam's, the small troll stared at us from the corner of the bedroom.

The next day, we drove a few hours to Glacier Beach. I had to stop at the gas station due to morning sickness, and even the bathrooms there were pristine compared to those in the U.S. On my knees, the white bathroom tiles sparkled. As a courtesy, I bought something at the gas station: Icelandic Skyer Strawberry Yogurt, my new go-to pregnancy craving.

When we arrived on Glacier Beach,

bundled-up tourists were taking pictures of the iconic ice chunks. A seal sunbathed on one of the floating glaciers, and tourists squealed with delight when it playfully flopped back into the water. We walked through the pitch-black rocky sand, admiring the contrast with the cloudy ocean water.

Nearby, a bride in a long silk gown posed next to her groom. I used to roll my eyes at bridal pictures, but now I envisioned our own. A rainbow shot across the sky, which caused the spectators to swoon. I wondered if Gautam would propose now or wait until we saw the northern lights. We would be returning home tomorrow, and there was no guarantee that the aurora would appear. I knew the ring was in his pocket, but I liked that he still wanted to make it a surprise for me.

Back in the modern hotel, we curled up beneath the crisp white covers and downloaded an aurora borealis tracker to notify us if the lights were noticeable. Throughout the night, my phone remained silent.

The next morning, I dragged my feet as we packed to leave the countryside. I was determined to see the lights on our drive into the city, so I kept my eyes peeled on the landscape, full of stark, century-old white churches. Right before we made it into Reykjavik, a green streak dashed across the sky.

"Is that it?" I nudged Gautam's shoulder and pointed out my window.

He pulled off Route One, and we jumped from the car. He got down on one knee.

"Will you be my wife and mother of my child?" he asked in a serious whisper. A car whizzed by us, making the proposal feel even more adventurous.

A wife. Being a mother felt natural, an instantaneous yes, but I couldn't imagine making a good wife. I'd spent my early twenties being terrified of love, and now I had to let myself feel it all. *To be someone's life partner. To have a child together. To raise a family.* So much responsibility, but I was complimented that someone like him saw so much potential in me.

This hesitation felt silly underneath the dancing lights. Love won.

"Yes," I said. He slid the diamond band onto my finger.

We watched the colorful streaks dancing across the sky, bundled up together on the hood of the car as my new diamond band sparkled under the green and orange hues of the northern lights.

Iceland's airport didn't have a direct flight to Philly, but it did to Washington, D.C. We spent the night at Gautam's sister's house in the City of Falls Church, a suburb of D.C., before returning to Philly. Komal was married with two young boys. As soon as I was through the door, I rushed to the powder room and fell to my knees. She knew our secret before Gautam revealed it to her later that night.

In the morning, I was the first person awake

in the colonial house. The sun leaked through the windows, and the glass patio doors revealed a wooden deck, vibrant green lawn, and glimpses of neighboring homes with a similar style. Besides the beauty, her home was warm and full of love. I loved that I felt just as comfortable with Gautam's family as I did with him.

Without my morning coffee routine, I settled for tea and heated the water to help my unsettled stomach.

As I poured a cup, sockless footsteps echoed down the hall. A moment later, Komal entered with a cozy sweater around her shoulders.

"Want one?" I asked, nodding to the tea.

"Sure," she replied, offering me a warm smile.

She was the first loved one who knew about the pregnancy and had experience being pregnant, too. I suddenly wanted to ask her a million questions about her boys and her experience.

"How have you been feeling?" she asked as she let her tea steep and darken.

"Not too bad," I said. Despite those anxious feelings of being a younger mother, I felt ready. I was already so connected with Gautam and our baby.

"First pregnancy?" she asked, adding milk to her tea. The spoon clattered as it swirled around her glass.

"Yes." I took a sip of tea, startled by the question since I didn't have any other children. I was naïve to the fact that many pregnancies don't result in a baby. I only knew one person who'd had a miscarriage, a high-school teacher who had confided in me about her pregnancy loss.

Looking back now, I long to once again have an easy answer to that question. When I started showing with my second pregnancy, my tongue would twist, and I never knew what to say. If I said no, I'd feel guilty. But the subject of my still-born daughter seemed to cause discomfort.

"Exciting," Komal said. "I'm here if you need anything."

"I'm going to take you up on your offer. None of my friends are expecting." Komal was easy to talk to; the words escaped out of my mouth.

"I can relate. I was in my early thirties with my boys, and most of my friends thought *that* was young."

"Wow." This made me feel a lot better. Suddenly my gag reflex kicked in. "Oh, excuse me," I said, slapping a hand over my mouth as I ran down the hallway.

"It'll all be worth it once you have that little baby in your arms!" she called after me.

CHAPTER FOUR

*I*t'll all be worth it once you have that little
baby in your arms. That sentence turned into
my guiding mantra when I found myself on the
bathroom floor again. And again. I heard it in
meetings when I sipped on ginger ale instead of
coffee. I heard it when hot tears streamed down
my face after a gentle suggestion to dress more
professionally at work. *It'll all be worth it once
you have that little baby in your arms.*

Dressing more professionally was a valid
suggestion; I didn't want to spend extra cash
to buy a new maternity work wardrobe as my
belly expanded over the months, so I wore baggy
clothes to the office. Although my family and
some friends knew by then and were as thrilled
as Gautam and I were about the baby, we decided
to wait until after the wedding to announce our
pregnancy more publicly.

I reached out to Komal to tell her what had
happened, and she emailed her mom network in
Northern Virginia to see if anyone would be inter-
ested in getting rid of their maternity clothes. I
wished I had my own mom network and longed

for the comfort of a community. None of my friends were expecting, let alone married.

On our next visit to Komal's, we went for a walk on the Washington and Old Dominion trail near her home. My mother-in-law joined us as well. I loved that we could take a break from the busy life inside the home and get outside on the trail. As we walked at a brisk pace, my mother-in-law asked about how my parents felt about their grandchild.

"They are excited," I said. "My mom is eager to babysit."

"Oh. I'm not feeling like that just yet," she said. She never refrained from speaking what was exactly on her mind, which I admired. She was a smart woman and had achieved her master's in physics in India. She married her husband, Lokesh, within months of meeting him and eventually set off for a life in America. Things were good, until Lokesh's sudden cancer diagnosis made her a widow. Gautam had been my age when he'd lost his father.

"Mom!" Komal exclaimed, totally mortified as she nudged her mother.

"It's totally fine," I replied, laughing at her honesty. I was used to it at this point. My one friend who had not been thrilled about my pregnancy early on was now on board with the idea. I felt like a professional at this point. I knew I'd find a way to get my mother-in-law excited to meet her grandchild.

"My parents were very surprised, too, at first," I added.

"I'll feel better once you're married," she replied. "I'm so happy my son is *finally* getting married." I caught a smile when she said that. She said that phrase often, over the phone to aunties, and even to strangers, like the jeweler.

"Of course," I said. "We will plan something special."

After the walk, Komal led me to her basement, where a big brown box of maternity clothes sat amidst toddler toys. "I picked these up for you today," she said. "Look how much stuff you got!"

"I'm speechless," I said, truly humbled that she had taken time out of her busy schedule to do this for me. "Thank you so much."

She went through the items with me—shirts, stretchy pants, and breastfeeding bras. Almost everything was designer: Loft, Destination Maternity, and some GAP pieces. A few items from the hospital had slipped in, too: jumbo pads, ice packs, and a pair of diaper-like underwear in a sealed plastic package.

"Oh, my—what's that?" I asked, giggling as I pointed to the gigantic underwear.

"Ugh, these, my friend, are post-childbirth undies."

Childbirth. There were so many things to learn about it: medicated vs. non-medicated, doulas, epidurals, Caesarean. The whole process seemed overwhelming.

Komal then added a few items from her own closet. She gingerly went through the clothes, relating her memories of them, such as her favorite pants and the forest-green shirt she'd worn when she'd given birth to her second son.

"What's it like? Did you have medication?" I asked.

"It's hard but doable. By the time I got to the hospital for both boys, I was always too far into labor to get the epidural."

"Are you sure you want me to have this?" I said as I placed my finger on the emerald-green shirt, the one she had given birth to her youngest in. Each item she gave me held a treasured memory for her.

"Yes," she said and smiled.

I glanced at the box in a different light, wondering why a mother would not want to hang onto clothes that had become such personal keepsakes. I understood the value of cleaning up and getting rid of a few items, but an entire box of clothes seemed off. The only exception would be if her pregnancy had only offered memories she'd rather forget.

I dismissed the thought. *Don't be silly*, I told myself. *Everyone lets go of things.*

From that day forward, I wore the maternity outfits, even though I had this ridiculous idea that they were bad luck or cursed. On the days I wore Komal's special hand-me-downs, I was much more at ease. My growing bump felt the love she had for her boys, and not another word about my clothes was spoken.

CHAPTER FIVE

"This won't work! Your bump is showing!" my grandmother exclaimed in her raspy voice. She had been a smoker, but she'd quit recently so she could meet her great-grandchild, and perhaps most importantly, catch the season finale of *Game of Thrones*. We had endeared her with the nickname "Gram of Thrones" due to her passion for the show.

I stood in my mother's bedroom, wearing a tight Herve Leger white dress that I had ordered online. By now, our immediate family finally knew about the pregnancy. My parents were supportive, stressed, and eager to be grandparents. My family was Catholic and Italian and felt things should be done the "proper" way; they wanted to keep the pregnancy a secret from the extended family until Gautam and I officially tied the knot.

"I think it's fine," I said, admiring how the skintight dress accentuated my growing curve.

"Won't a tight dress hurt the baby?" my grandmother asked as her wrinkled hands tugged at the material.

"Oh, Mom, cut it out," said my mother. "It's beautiful."

I changed out of the dress and caught a chill. I often did in my parent's townhouse, which they had moved to after becoming empty nesters. The townhouse backed into one of the oldest cemeteries in my hometown, and the graveyard cats often brawled and shrieked as they fought. My mother denied that the house was haunted, but she often had dreams about those buried behind the house, including the town's founding members. She never slept in the house alone from her discomfort, and if my dad was traveling out of town, she would spend the night at my grandmother's house nearby.

I spent the night at my parents', and I had a dream that a boy walked into my bedroom. He looked nine or ten, with dark hair and big round eyes. But when I looked down, I noticed he had blue feet.

"What happened?' I asked him, but he vanished.

My spiritualist called the boy a frozen baby. Such babies come to earth to help heal past-life trauma. That didn't entirely resonate with me. I didn't want my baby to have past-life baggage, but I was certain I was having a boy. In Iceland, I was so confident that I'd bought a powder-blue baby bib with a puffin on it that said *Iceland* instead of a gender-neutral one. It was the baby's first international trip, after all.

But a few weeks later I was taking a shower and felt a jolt, and the small voice said, *You're having a girl.* I clenched my belly, thinking of what a strange message that was. I didn't know what went on when a baby's soul came into this world, but something seemed off, like things had changed and were not going according to the original plan.

Gautam and I were married in mid-December in the middle of a snowstorm in Philadelphia. The traffic lights blew out, and we barely made it to City Hall on time for pictures. We took photos outside the courthouse beforehand, and I became irritated in my open-heel shoes as the cold slush and snow froze my feet. I thought I'd get frost-bite by the time our photographer finished. "Cold feet," I joked to Gautam. Most of my family couldn't get there on time due to traffic, but we got married anyway. I accidentally tried to slide Gautam's ring on the wrong finger as I said, "I do."

After, we had family over and ate hoagies and pizza. My grandfather filled my champagne flute with sparkling grape juice. My husband's cousin had a newborn, and Gautam asked if I'd like to hold the baby. I froze—the newborn, in his mother's arms, was so perfect and small.

"Go on. You can hold him," my new husband insisted.

It felt like a test, and I was worried it would show that I had no clue how to hold a newborn. I was the first in my small family and friend group to have a baby. The only newborn I'd held was my brother when he was a baby. I wanted to save my next newborn hold for our baby.

"Let him sleep," I said with a smile, although I felt I had offended the mother.

When the guests left, Gautam reserved a hotel room down the street to make the night special, and we ordered room service. We rented a movie that we didn't watch, and instead, we made love. In the morning, I woke up from our first night together as a married couple feeling like a different person. Most of all, I was ready to have our baby.

Even after we got married, I kept the pregnancy a secret from many. I didn't make any posts on social media, and I didn't tell friends outside of my close circle. I felt superstitious about posting something for a larger audience. I worried that if I did, I'd jinx myself. It all seemed too good to be true.

The genetic testing confirmed we were having a little girl. Although I had an uneasy feeling, I stuffed it into the back of my mind. I had to be strong for her. We were having a *girl*. There is something pure about having a little girl. You want to protect her, but at the same time, you want her to be like you. I was her biggest fan. I was going to match our outfits, not all the time but *sometimes*. I'd brush her hair every night and hope that after reading to her enough, she would fall in love with it like I had. I would sing to her, although I had a terrible voice. I would make her laugh, and I would make her realize she would grow to be a powerful, smart woman who had the world at her fingertips.

I often daydreamed about turning into a stay-at-home mom like my mother. The nineties seemed like a golden age to raise children. I was one of three siblings, the middle child, and I never went to daycare. When I was sick at school, she'd come and get me and take care of me. She poured her entire life into our well-being. My father worked his tail off as a salesman to make it possible for her to stay home with us.

I knew a few young couples with kids, and with the cost of daycare, it often made sense for one partner to stay home. My position at my company was entry level. I dreamed that staying home would somehow work out for me, especially if my parents pulled through on their childcare promise. In my new bright-pink planner—pink for a girl—I jotted down fantasies about future hobbies as a stay-at-home mother: take writing classes, go to yoga, learn to cook, and take our baby for long walks in the park.

But I knew I had to work. I had student loans. I had an entire career ahead of me. I still can't pinpoint why I so often fantasized about not working and being with our baby, unless it was simply that a love fierce enough to drop everything to be with our child danced through my growing body.

CHAPTER SIX

My pregnancy craving was lemons. At first, I craved lemonade. When we'd go out to eat, I'd often order off the kid's menu and get buttered noodles and a large glass of lemonade. To my dismay, there were a surprising number of restaurants that didn't serve lemonade. To compensate, I'd get lemon water.

I'd also bring lemons from the market with me to work. I'd slice them in the morning to drop in my chilled water. Once, I forgot to slice the lemons, so I used a knife from the office pantry to do it. When no one was looking, I took a bite of the sweet and sour lemon. I remembered how the captain of my high school cross-country team used to brag about eating lemons. I could never understand how anyone could do it, yet there I was.

My mouth watered. It was my little secret. I'd tell Laila when she was older. I could imagine her scrunched face giggling when I said, "I once ate a plain lemon when you were in my belly."

One night, I gasped for air like I was underwater, but when I awoke, I was in the dark bedroom. Even with my eyes open, my head was spinning. Gautam woke up right away. I couldn't catch my breath.

"You okay?" he asked as he flicked on the light switch, which was near his side of the bed.

"Call the doctor," I said and reached for the stale glass of water on the bedside table. I had poured it before going to bed, but it was better than nothing. I drank it.

When I called the hospital, the after-hours nurse said, "If you feel something is wrong, please come in."

I knew something was wrong; a sick feeling bubbled up in my gut.

The doorman called us a taxi, and I felt like this was it. Something had happened to my baby.

When we arrived at the hospital, the staff directed us to the labor and delivery wing. I checked in at a small corridor before the actual delivery floor.

I was convinced something was going downhill with the pregnancy.

The nurse came in and pulled the curtain around us. She checked me in and checked my vitals. The doctor conducted an exam, and I was healthy. Nothing was wrong.

"Have you thought about talking to someone?" the doctor suggested.

"I can. I have a therapist from college," I said, feeling defeated.

I'd thought it was a real emergency. From

experience, I knew anxiety could manifest physically with me, but the intuition that something was wrong had been so powerful. Still, I knew I wanted to avoid false alarms like these in the future.

Near the end of January, I had my twenty-week visit at the end of my workday. We were eager to see our baby girl on the big ultrasound screen, and I wanted the extra reassurance. I'd only seen her once, at the eight-week visit, and she'd been so small, kidney-bean sized. I had proudly carried those early ultrasound photos around in my purse, taking them all the way to Washington, D.C., to show my in-laws. But today we were going to see a much bigger baby. I'd have a better photo to share.

The appointment was in the maternal-fetal medicine wing at the hospital I would give birth at. I had it on my list to take a tour of the labor and delivery wing. In the lobby, some pregnant mothers looked concerned, and I wondered if any of them had high-risk conditions. I was thankful that my pregnancy, aside from morning sickness, had been easy and low-risk.

In the ultrasound room, we watched our baby girl glow on the screen. It was like watching a movie, but we were the ones writing the story. Gautam and I stared at the screen in awe.

"Do you know the gender?" the technician asked.

"Yes," Gautam said as he grasped my hand

tightly. His desire to be a father still made my heart soar.

"Good. I don't want to give away any surprises. Her heartbeat looks great. Did you pick a name yet?" the technician asked as she zoomed in on the baby's heartbeat.

"Laila," I replied. Gautam was transfixed by the ghostly white image of our daughter floating around the dark screen.

"She's so beautiful," he said.

While studying Urdu, I'd read the famous story of Laila and Majnun, often described as the Romeo and Juliet of South Asia, although their tale is centuries older. The star-crossed lovers could never be together, and Majnun's obsessive devotion to Laila drove him insane. Gautam loved the name when I suggested it.

"Baby is being stubborn for me today," the technician said, pressing the wand harder into my belly. "We will need a few more pictures. Why don't you try going to the bathroom? That should get her moving."

I waddled over to the single bathroom and thought nothing of the strange suggestion. Surely, if anything was wrong, our medical team would have said something.

"C'mon, Laila, move around so we can see you," I whispered as I rubbed my belly.

Back in the room with an empty bladder, I gave Gautam a reassuring smile. The technician brought out the transvaginal ultrasound to get better images. "Let's give this another shot," she said, carefully searching the screen.

I tried to relax, imagining robotic sex as the contraption probed my insides. Gautam seemed to know precisely what I was thinking, and we both tried to refrain from laughter. I bit the inside of my cheek so I wouldn't erupt in giggles. He gripped my hand. The technician scanned each part with ease, revealing our baby's left knee, right knee, elbows, brain. When each was identified correctly, the area would light up like a video game, all to the beat of the printer's synchronous hum. As the technician finished, the doctor entered the room.

"She looks great. Have you been feeling her kicks yet?" she asked.

"Only little flutters. When do I need to start tracking them?"

"That'll be the third trimester. I bet you'll feel them more soon."

The technician handed me a stack of ultrasound images, and I tucked them carefully away in my purse, making a note to order a photo album to keep all of Laila's pictures.

A few years later, during my second pregnancy, I would ask again about Laila's limited movement on the day of the scan. The doctor looked at me with sad eyes, as if I were an obsessive detective who couldn't give up a case. She said that Laila might have just been sleeping. Or maybe it was an early sign that something was wrong. *There was no way of knowing and nothing you could have done.*

CHAPTER SEVEN

The previous Valentine's, we'd gone out to a bar in South Philly. We'd found it ironic to eat buttery crab legs and wings with beer instead of sharing a romantic candlelit dinner. But this year, with some wedding money, Gautam went above and beyond to plan an elaborate babymoon in Sedona, Arizona. He'd originally picked Paris.

"Paris? I want to go, but I don't want to travel that far with the baby," I said. Visiting Paris would have been a dream, though. I wanted Laila's middle name to be Paris, although no one else liked the name. I had been inspired by Shakespearean names; Paris was the one who vied for Juliet's love. In college, my pet mouse became pregnant by a stray house mouse. I watched as, over the next month, her belly expanded and she burrowed in her nest of hay, preparing for her children. They were born furless and bright red, but once they grew their distinctive and multi-colored fur coats, I named them after Shakespearean characters, Ophelia, Malvolio, Sebastian, Juliet, and Hamlet, before releasing them into the field behind the dorm house.

"It would be the perfect place for a baby-moon," he said. "Endless macaroons."

"I know, but what if something happens?" I said. "There was that recent terrorist attack, too." I grimaced as I imagined another attack. It was decided—we would go to Sedona, and we would take Laila to Paris when she was older.

As we drove down the highway in a rented Mustang convertible, I pointed out familiar landmarks. For my first job out of college, I'd worked remotely for a company based in Phoenix, and once a year, we'd head to Scottsdale for the holiday party. Gautam and I stopped in Old Town Scottsdale for an early dinner, and I had flashbacks of carefree, drunken nights, dry sand, and wheeling around in the golf carts that served as taxis to make it back to the hotel.

After dinner, we drove until the sun went down on Route 179 and the dark, winding roads that eventually brought us all the way to Sedona.

The morning sun broke over our view of Bell Rock from the hotel window. I could see why the place was a spiritual hub. A reiki practitioner had told me New Age mystics flocked to the land, believing that Sedona was a spiritual vortex. The land was said to be sacred and energetic.

Before we left for our first hike, Gautam stopped at the concierge desk.

"Do you have any recommendations for easy hiking trails? My wife is expecting," he said with a proud smile on his face.

"Of course." The concierge handed us a map of easy local trails, which Gautam tucked into his jacket pocket. He was an avid hiker who would easily scale the top of Cathedral Rock, so I found it endearing that he'd take the easy nature walks with me. His thoughtfulness was another sign that he'd be a good father, a protective father, the kind who would always put the well-being of his child before his own.

The Arizona winter was cool and crisp, like spring weather back in the Northeast. We took long walks along the red-rock trails, and Gautam held my canister of water. I exchanged smiles with other pregnant mothers partaking in the same adventure. We saw a couple with their baby in a chest carrier, and I gripped Gautam's hand in excitement, knowing that our baby girl would be with us soon and we'd go on adventures as a family.

Beneath the desert sun, my nesting instincts were triggered. I filled a jar with the orange sand, which is said to be energetic. I planned to keep it in our baby's future nursery, along with the evil eye I'd purchased from a New Age crystal store to ward off any bad energy. Before we set up a nursery, I would insist on clearing the apartment of any unwanted presences, thinking of my own childhood and the scary shapes I had seen in the dark.

At a day spa in Sedona, we dressed in white terrycloth bathrobes, and I was amused by how much we looked like newlyweds. I sipped on lemon water, and Gautam had seltzer as we reclined on the lounge chairs on the small patio, waiting for our massages. I was too worried to get a real massage, so I opted for a Reiki/chakra clearing session.

The practitioner was kind and had a bunch of crystals and rose quartz out on the massage table. I asked her which crystals would be best for the nursery, and she confirmed that the ones I had bought would be perfect for protecting the space from any unwanted spirits. Then I sat down on the massage table, careful not to recline too far, and the practitioner brought out a few pillows for additional comfort.

She breathed deeply and said a few "Oms" to connect to the Reiki spirit as she lit sage and waved a bird feather around, and then she glided her hands over my body. Often in Reiki sessions, my ability to see things is heightened when I shut my eyes. This time, my vision began with me at the bottom of a lake, looking up into the starry night sky. I saw trees circling the lake and a full moon. Then I moved into the future and saw Laila as an adult. Her black hair was tied back in a bun, and she wore a tailored business suit. She was working in politics in D.C. Who knows? She could even have been president. All of this made so much sense. I was so connected to her because she was a very special soul, going to do such big things in the world, a true leader. *It'll all be worth it once you have that little baby in your arms.*

On one of our final days, Gautam and I took a trip to Lake Powell. We drove with the top down along the jet-black highways, following the roads deep into the intoxicating landscape. In the middle of this long stretch of desert and cacti, the

Coconino National Forest surprised us by offering towering pine trees capped with fresh snow.

We stopped at a stand alongside the highway, and I bought handwoven sage from the Navajo nation to add to my spiritual safety collection. At the lake, we kayaked for miles through the canyon with a few other couples, who paddled along beside us. Insistent on protecting the pregnancy, Gautam took care of the rowing while I sat behind him and ran my hands through the cold, clear water and the stone walls. With its exposed red rock layers and light-bending slots, the canyon surrounding Lake Powell resembled the landscape of Mars. Fossil imprints marked some of the walls.

In the hotel, we stripped off our soaked shirts and pants. I paused for a moment in my bra and damp underwear and posed in the corner of the hotel room near the window.

"What are you doing?' Gautam asked with an amused look on his face.

"Take a picture!"

"Seriously?" The hotel room was a mess—our wet clothes hung on a chair , and a picture of Antelope Canyon hung in the background.

I explained to him that I didn't have any maternity pictures, and now that my bump was large, I wanted to have one to remember how big and stretch-mark-free my belly was.

"Sure," he said with a shrug.

That photo was nothing glamorous, but it remains one of my favorite pregnancy pictures from before Laila passed. When I showed the picture to a friend after her death, they said they didn't realize I had been that far along.

On our last morning, we shared the same dreams of exploring the mountainous landscape and getting lost in the red rocks. Black ravens lined the fence, Cathedral Rock loomed in the distance, and a mist had settled over the landscape. I waved my phone around for cell service to check in on my family, worried that those birds signified death. When I got a connection, I discovered that no one had died, but I couldn't shake the feeling I got from those dark eyes and lush black feathers watching over us. I rubbed my belly with a sense of foreboding.

One last thing that happened just days before Laila died. At twenty-six weeks gestation, I tended to Ernie in our apartment, clipping off his stale yellow leaves. Suddenly a voice seemed to whisper in my ear, *Your baby has died*. I looked around the room, but no one was around. Did the plant speak? I decided it was anxiety, a manifestation of my innermost fear.

No, there was one final occurrence. My older sister called me, scared, convinced that she had a ghost in her rowhome in Manayunk. I was the one family and friends called whenever they sensed an otherworldly presence, because I could try to decode their messages and visits, especially after my Reiki training. I asked my sister to precisely describe the event. I loved piecing together ghost stories and finding meaning, especially when it wasn't happening to me directly.

I found it ironic that my big sister was the one calling me to calm her down. In our house growing up, the previous owner had died in a sudden car crash down the road. I'd often see him roaming the hallways in his boxers, and I'd run into her room and squeeze into her twin bed. She'd welcome me into her room, and we'd snuggle together until I felt safe.

"Tell me everything," I said, intrigued.

"I was in my room, and I had a chill. I heard the hallway floorboards creak, but no one was home. Then my Bluetooth speaker suddenly started playing a nursery song. *Mary had a little lamb, little lamb, little lamb*. It was terrifying." My sister said breathlessly.

For some reason, I told her not to worry. Comforting words left my lips: "I bet you it was Laila visiting you already, excited to meet her aunt!"

Only later did I realize that I was talking about Laila like she was a ghost and had already died.

Chapter Eight

An early March snowstorm didn't warrant a cab ride for our half-mile walk to the office. I applied a thick layer of Vaseline to my face and lips to help prevent windburn. Gautam kneeled to help lace up my snow boots; bending over had become too difficult with my budding third-trimester belly. We left early so we could take our time. I avoided the obvious icy spots and clung to Gautam as if my life depended on it. The snowy, wet wind stung my face, piercing the thick layer of cream.

"I'm going to be late for the appointment tomorrow. Will you be able to get there on your own?" Gautam asked, his warm breath creating a small cloud over his face. I tightened my grip on his arm. There was something romantic about how the weather brought us so physically close despite all of the layers of gear wrapped around us.

"Totally fine," I said as I tried to ignore the voice I'd heard in my head. Again, I shuddered, but I knew it was my own nerves. Gautam had shuffled his busy schedule to be at every visit so far. This was the first time he wouldn't be there on time, and I couldn't expect he'd be able to make it to every visit.

"I'll get there as soon as I can. I would reschedule, but it's for fundraising," he added. He often helped me with financial literacy. Fundraising was critical in the seed round for Series A. The more money the company raised, the more likely it was that he would get an actual salary instead of only equity.

"I know you will, but don't stress yourself out," I said and squeezed his hand through my glove. I refrained from teasing him that he couldn't make it on time; we joked that my nagging had already caused him to develop early gray hairs.

As an empty beer can rolled down the sidewalk, he slowed his pace and carefully guided my ungainly body around it. "Let me know how your day goes. I'm here if you need me."

My shoulders relaxed as he gently kissed the top of my forehead. The smell of his aftershave soothed me for a moment.

"I know," I replied, wishing for something stronger than a scent to erase my concern.

I rubbed my belly as I scanned my emails. Reading the report on my desk had been useless—the words had bled together—so now I was trying to clear my email. I figured I should be able to handle that, at least. But a growing concern looped through my mind with each one scanned. I couldn't shake that voice: *Your baby has died.* I needed to give my OB-GYN a call, but I feared I'd sound like a lunatic: *Hi there. A voice in my head says my baby died. Can I move my appointment to today?*

I closed my office doors and dialed the number, which I knew by heart. Whenever I called the doctor's office, the nurse brought up something personal and embarrassing, and I would have to confirm or deny it. *No, I'm not constipated. No, I don't have vaginal bleeding.* And so on. As I described my anxiousness to the nurse on the other line, I clenched my right hand around a stress ball with a giant smiley face on it.

"When was the last time you felt your baby kick?" the nurse asked as she went through what I imagined to be her list of routine questions.

I paused and rubbed my hand across my belly. I hadn't felt Laila's daily flutters this morning. "I can't remember. She may have kicked last night." At my last visit, my doctor had said it was still too early to conduct kick counts. The baby's kicks wouldn't become trackable until twenty-eight weeks into the pregnancy, as was additionally noted in all my hospital discharge forms in bold print, and I was at twenty-six weeks.

There was a pause on the other end of the line, and I wondered if I needed to explain myself more to the nurse. Maybe she didn't realize what gestational week I was in or that I had an appointment tomorrow morning.

"You haven't felt any kicks today? Please drink something sugary and try to count kicks. We don't have any openings today. You should head to the hospital," she suggested.

"I will. Thanks for checking," I said, unsure as I tried to stay calm. I kept pumping the stress ball in my fist.

As the nurse advised, I needed to eat something sweet to coax Laila to kick and get rid of the fog I felt. I pawed through my desk drawer for a candy—the sugar sometimes got a rise out of her—but my stock had run dry. Then, way in the back, beneath some stray papers, I found a lump. I relaxed. One Jolly Rancher. I unpeeled the plastic and popped it into my mouth. Then I strummed my fingers along my belly. *Nothing.*

I didn't want to panic again and have an embarrassing false alarm like last time. I confided in my friends about the decline in fetal movement, and they reassured me that my baby was probably snuggled up in a different position, and that kick counts can vary so early on. I could imagine it now: I'd rush over in the middle of a snowstorm only to get another referral to a psychologist. Remembering what I'd learned in therapy, I breathed deeply.

A million other reasons to keep calm filled my mind. I didn't want to leave work early today and tomorrow since I'd already visited the hospital. And the money, of course. A visit to the emergency room would cost more than a hundred dollars, while my regular monthly appointment would be completely covered by insurance. Saving a hundred dollars could add up to a few cases of diapers or other expensive baby products.

I went to refill my water cup at the cooler on

my way to the restroom.

"Are you doing okay?" my senior colleague asked as he breezed by.

"It's strange. I can't remember the last time Laila kicked," I admitted as I sipped on the cold water.

"She must have kicked when you were sleeping," he said as he paused to refill his own water cup. "Trust me. I have five kids."

I hadn't thought of that and was relieved. "Thanks for that."

In the restroom, as I splashed cold water on my face, I experienced a huge swish across my belly. I was so relieved that I wanted to cry. Our baby was fine. It was a powerful kick, too, not her usual butterfly flutters near my bladder. In the previous weeks, I'd begun to imagine the butterflies were real, like the ones I'd raised as a child with my kindergarten classmates. We'd watched the caterpillars go through metamorphosis in the bright plastic contraption our teacher kept on the classroom bookshelf. By the spring, we'd released the orange-winged Monarchs into the soccer field behind the playground. I'd chased after them, but with their large, clunky wings, the butterflies couldn't yet fly fast enough to leave me behind. I couldn't wait for Laila to make her own memories.

I was calmer now and messaged Gautam, relieved that we worked in the same building; his physical proximity helped ease me. I met him at the elevator banks.

"What do you think? I can go to the hospital today with you." He scanned my face for any hint of false alarm.

I took a deep breath, trying to brush off my concern. Pregnant people are hormonal lunatics, right? I'm sure we'd laugh about my nerves later on, once we had our sweet baby in our arms.

"No, I can wait for tomorrow. I felt her kick, and I bet I'll feel her again once I grab a Gatorade from the store," I said, feeling mature. I had overcome my anxiety.

I fumbled with the zipper on my winter jacket, but it was too snug. Gautam helped me as he fastened each button, one by one, and he rubbed my belly. Outside, the snow gathered in a thick layer. By the end of the day, the city was silent with snowfall.

CHAPTER NINE

Snowfall melted on the salted streets. Like the day before, Gautam walked by my side on our way to work. I felt better today. The calm voice of my therapist rang in my head: *Of course you're ready to be a mother. Twenty-five isn't that young. All mothers get worried. All mothers feel unprepared.*

After my last meeting wrapped up, I had the rest of the day off to head to the doctor's. I slid off my flats and put on my snow boots. Then I grabbed my purse and left the building. It was freezing outside for March.

Philadelphia's cross streets are named after trees. We lived off Walnut, and before that, I couch surfed on Spruce in college. I headed down Cherry until I reached the Four Seasons Hotel. Taxicabs were lined up out front, and when I waved, one of the drivers pulled out of line for me. I opened the door and wiggled into the back seat. The worst part of getting bigger was all the wiggling I had to do when sliding into a car.

At the medical facility, I cracked a smile when I saw my father in the lobby. I was so thrilled to have him there that I ran up and hugged him. I'd mentioned to him the other day about my nerves, but I had never expected him to come to my appointment. I felt very silly.

"You didn't need to do this, Dad. Gautam will be here soon," I said, although I felt better not being alone. I knew he had come from New Jersey, a half-hour's drive, to meet me. It reminded me of how, when I used to run cross-country, he'd make it a priority to come to every race with my mother despite his busy work schedule.

"It's over the bridge. Don't worry about it," he replied. While South Jersey and Philly are close to each other, those raised in South Jersey often talk about going "over the bridge" to get to Philly. The main way to cross the Delaware River is the blue Ben Franklin Bridge, which not only has a toll, but crazy traffic and drivers shouting at each other. Having to "go over the bridge" to get into the city is often a production, and my dad was downplaying it. Either way, I was excited to have him there and proud to have his support. I was eager to introduce him to my doctors and show him what exceptional care I was getting.

We sat next to each other in the waiting room, and I pried out my copy of *The Master and Margarita*. I had a goal of finally reading this Russian classic before the baby arrived. One of my friends from college had raved about it, but when I'd tried to read it, I'd gotten lost in the text. I struggled to fully grasp the fantastical story about the devil arriving in Moscow, raising hell on earth with his infamous talking black cat.

After a brief wait, the nurse called us back. In the medical room, my technician revealed a strained smile when she listened for the baby's heartbeat. "This happens sometimes with the Doppler," she said. "Let's order an ultrasound."

I acted like this was typical, doing my best to reassure my father as I waddled down the hallway. He stayed close behind me as we followed the nurse.

In the ultrasound room, I wondered if my insurance would cover it this time around. I'd just received the thousand-dollar charge from my twenty-week ultrasound. Since I hadn't yet hit my two-thousand-dollar deductible, the potential cost weighed heavily on my mind.

While we waited for the doctor, Gautam walked into the room. I couldn't believe the timing; I'd expected him to arrive much later.

"Sorry I'm late," he said, looking sharp in a tailored suit. I wondered how his meeting had gone, but before I could bring it up, he asked, "What's going on?" He stood by the door like a security guard.

"The doctor needs to do an ultrasound. The Doppler wasn't working," my dad replied. I nodded and gave Gautam a reassuring smile.

A doctor I'd never met entered the room and said, "Let me have a look here." As she tied her hair back and washed her hands, the three of us didn't say anything. I was sure they were thinking the same thing I was: *Why is the doctor doing my ultrasound?*

She sat on her rolling stool and reached for

the device. I didn't want to make eye contact with her, or anyone, so I stared at the cork ceiling. The room suddenly felt heavy; it seemed to press down on me, forcing the air from my lungs and making it hard to breathe.

"I have bad news," the doctor said matter-of-factly. "The baby is dead."

I kept my gaze on the panels above me and decided that I wanted to die, too. There was no life without my baby. The doctor leaned close to me and added, "I'm so sorry."

"Oh? This happened last time," Gautam said in disbelief. "Laila doesn't like to cooperate sometimes. Can we try again tomorrow?"

The doctor put her hand on my arm. Ice cold. "If there were a heartbeat, I'd be able to hear it."

I squirmed in my seat. "So, is there medication for that? A stronger ultrasound to detect the heartbeat?" I thought we might need another vaginal transponder to send little shocks into my womb like last time.

"There's nothing else we can do, I'm afraid. Your baby is dead."

I recoiled at the doctor's words, delivered again in a flat voice. No emotion. Then I wondered if she always spoke in a monotone. Even if my baby were alive, I could see this doctor delivering good news in the same tone of voice. I pictured a delivery room scenario in which the doctor filed her nails as I screamed in pain, pausing only to catch the baby as she slid out and then tossing her quickly back to me.

I wished Dr. C were there. I trusted her. I knew

she would help us.

As if reading my mind, Gautam asked, "Is Dr. C here today?"

The doctor checked the schedule and told us Dr. C was working in the labor and delivery wing. "She will meet you at the hospital if you decide to go today."

Gautam grabbed my hand, but I didn't notice. There was no way I could look at the screen. The last time we had seen Laila, she'd had a heartbeat. She'd been alive. And healthy. And growing. Now looking at the screen felt like looking into a casket.

I wanted to crawl out of my skin. My bones rattled as if I were standing on a transit platform while a train thundered by. All those months of preparing for my baby, wondering what Laila would look like, who she'd grow up to be . . . all snatched from my hands.

"If we'd gone to the hospital sooner, could we have saved her?" Gautam asked. His deceased father was a nephrologist, which made him well versed in translating medical complications.

The doctor shook her head and explained with a sad look, "If you'd come in earlier, we only could have induced labor—same options as today. For gestational death, there's no way to save a baby. It happens in seconds. There's nothing you could have done. Please remember that." Her eyes looked serious. I didn't know it then, but she was telling me this to help me navigate the blame and guilt.

"But I felt a kick today," I said, "a strong one."

Beyond the door, the busy staff rushed through the halls, the echoing clicks of their footsteps as they tended to real mothers providing proof that the world around me was still spinning. I'd been booted out of motherhood and felt dejected, like a phony, as Holden Caulfield says in *The Catcher in the Rye*. Perhaps this was the biggest sign of all that I was too young to be a mother. Maybe I deserved all of this. Yes, I was being punished.

"Sometimes women experience movement, what feels like kicks after the baby dies," she added, offering no explanation as to why this occurs. "You can head to the hospital now. Or some people like to wait and deliver naturally."

She sounded like she was underwater. I was frozen. How was I supposed to answer? I still hadn't accepted that my baby was dead.

"Do you need more time to process?" she said, still speaking in her stoic tone.

I still couldn't move. No words surfaced because I wasn't going to accept any of those choices. *No, I don't want to head to the hospital now. No, I don't want to wait and deliver a stillborn baby naturally. No, I don't need more time to process. What I need, more than anything, is for you to repeat the ultrasound and hear my baby's heartbeat. I need you to tell me everything is going to be okay.*

I remembered watching an episode of *Animal Planet* over the winter in which a mother elephant dragged her dead, dehydrated baby elephant with her, trying to keep up with the herd. After a few hours, she had to let go of the baby. The mother had prioritized her own survival. *Save the baby or save the mother.*

Afterwards, Gautam had told me he thought he had to make a choice in that room. *Save the baby or save the mother.*

"I'd like to go now," I asserted. My body, which had felt like a vessel of life mere moments earlier, now felt dangerous, like a sinking ship. I wanted to deliver. I wanted to feel safe again in my body. I thought that all I had to do was get through the childbirth and then it'd all be over. I was very wrong.

Gautam clenched my hand harder and nodded in agreement.

"Okay," she said. The rest of her words came in waves. "We'll call the hospital . . . head to the seventh floor . . . delivery center." The doctor's last words, the delivery center, rang eerily in my ear. I felt so unsettled that I sprang to my feet, determined to control something. Anything.

I walked out of the room and asked the front-desk clerk for parking validation for my father.

"That'll be five dollars," the clerk added. I wondered if she knew my baby was dead, because she didn't ask me about scheduling a follow-up appointment. As I robotically pulled a crisp five-dollar bill from my wallet, my hand grazed the blood-red cover of *The Master and Margarita*. The devil's cat on the cover suddenly looked terrifying and ominous.

⁓⁓⁓

Gautam rushed home to throw together an

overnight bag for our unplanned hospital stay. I'd always imagined those months and what I would pack for our time in the maternity ward . . . the loose-fitting clothes, the baby's going-home outfit, and soft, pre-washed muslin swaddles for my newborn. Now the packing was left to the discretion of my grief-stricken husband. It didn't matter what he packed. Nothing would comfort me.

I pushed through the heavy doors into the labor and delivery wing with my father's arms around my shoulders. My mother was on her way. When my father had called her, I'd heard her howl over the phone, floored with shock and sorrow. I couldn't imagine the disappointment of my mother-in-law and Komal; the plan had been for them to take the train from D.C. when I was in labor with a living child, not a deceased one.

When we arrived at check-in, a nurse ushered me back. As we entered my hospital room, Dr. C was waiting for me even though she'd already finished her shift. Years later, when I was scheduled for induction with my second daughter, she greeted me in the hospital room she'd birthed her own child in.

"I'm so sorry," she said as she rubbed my shoulder, showing far more compassion than the other doctor had offered. Tears formed in her eyes, and a wave of sadness hit me. I realized for the first time that my baby's death made other people sad, too, even people outside our family.

Dr. C settled me into the room, sat with me, and asked if I needed anything. I wanted her to stay, but I knew it was an impossible ask.

Then she explained, "You're in good hands here. The midwife will go over arrangements."

The pale-faced midwife stood behind her like a shadow, studying me with her large, round eyes.

When Dr. C left, the midwife rubbed my upper thigh. It almost seemed erotic, and I would still think she had been hitting on me if it hadn't been for the Lamaze technique I would read about years later. Just as I'd expected a midwife to be, she had a mythical quality. She was someone more sophisticated mothers would ask to guide their delivery. I had wanted the most direct route. I didn't care for homebirths, acupuncture, doulas, or birth photographers. I only wanted our baby.

"What are your preferences for funeral arrangements, photos, keepsake boxes, and autopsy reports?" she asked as she kneaded her fingers into my thigh.

"I don't think I have a preference," I said as an image of a tiny coffin appeared in the back of my mind—the thought of something so obscene made me nauseous. Her warm hands pressed harder, kneading me into my hospital bed as the soft waves of her brunette hair fell across her face.

"No problem. You have time. Do you want to hold the baby?"

I wondered how such a calm woman could talk of such dark things with such ease and professionalism.

I said no to everything the midwife asked me. I thought she'd be relieved—it would mean less work for her. I'd spent all of those months dreaming about being a young mother, and now my baby was being taken from me. I wanted Laila to be the first newborn I held, but I was scared. *A funeral? Pictures? Pictures of a lifeless baby? What does a lifeless baby look like? How small would the baby be?*

The pretty midwife's face sank with disappointment. "Let's wait until your husband gets back to review those final wishes. I don't want you to regret anything. Most mothers do if they don't spend time and bond with the baby."

Bond more. I couldn't see the purpose of connecting to my baby when she was already gone; it felt like a cruel joke. I felt cheated. Why would I want to feel *more* pain than this? At the same time, the idea of mothers regretting things in a shitty circumstance made me feel very sad. I didn't want to be a regretful mother, but I was terrified.

She kept rubbing my upper thigh to calm me, but my thoughts remained heavy. I was new to everything, nervous and scared, and it felt more comfortable to remain unattached. Saying no to the midwife felt like the only power I had left.

I then thought about giving birth. I still hadn't taken my Labor 101 class. It was scheduled for the following weekend, and I made a mental note to cancel it. With how things were going, I imagined myself centuries ago, bleeding to death in a long white nightgown after one of my many attempts to give the king a son. I imagined the midwife telling the king that I had died during the delivery and so had the baby. I thought of how angry the king would be at the news, how he'd nearly strangle the midwife for her failure to save either of us.

And then Gautam walked in, looking disheveled. He had changed into casual clothes, and he carried an overnight bag for us. His usually warm bronze skin now looked chalky white as he stood as close as possible to the hospital bed.

The midwife explained the arrangements again in her patient and gentle voice as if I were a child who hadn't been paying attention. Gautam surprised me. He said yes to all her questions . . . and wanted to hold the baby.

My face warmed with embarrassment. I didn't feel responsible enough to make these important decisions. Without him, I'd have been lost. He was right. This would be our only chance to be with our baby.

When the midwife left, I turned to him. "I'm scared to hold the baby."

"If you want, I can hold her. You don't need to."

He seemed so strong, but the idea made me weak.

My sister arrived at the hospital and noted that the door to our private room held a leaf with a teardrop on it, which, I learned later, signified to the staff that I would be delivering a stillborn.

"When I walked in, the staff thought that I was the one in labor," she said as she tried to get a smile from me. "I should lose some weight," she added as she tugged at her hips.

It worked. My parents softened as they

watched us interact. My brother still didn't know yet; he was in college and had final exams this week. Later on, when he found out that my parents had kept this event from him, he'd yelled, "If anything ever happens to *my* sister, you have to let me know!"

My sister had brought my favorite pregnancy cravings from the convenience store. The various candies and sweets didn't elicit a mouthwatering response from me anymore. The little one in my belly who had once danced at those foods now remained still.

Everyone except Gautam stepped out of the room when the nurse arrived to insert the cervix softener. My sister left shortly after, but my parents stayed.

When the mild cramps started, the nurse injected me with an IV full of pain medication, and I let the morphine work its way into my bloodstream. I let it help me disappear.

⁂

What really pushed my great-grandmother to death was the passing of her second daughter. "No parent should outlive their child," she told me. I had heard her say that before, and now she was saying it again with her other daughter. At 101 years old, my great-grandmother had health concerns as well, but she kept saying before her death how her heart had been broken. *Parents shouldn't outlive their children.*

Before Hilda died, my mother shared that she had hallucinated a fat tabby cat on the edge of her bed. With her history of clairvoyance, I was certain that hallucinations were a sign of imminent death. And while I didn't want to live without my baby, I felt very afraid of death coming after me, too. After hours of labor cramps (despite the heavy opioids), I stood guard for hallucinations. In my mind, they were the ticket to the Other Side. If I saw anything, anything, I would ring the nurse and make sure my vitals were fine. In my heavily sedated mind, this made the most sense.

I tried to read, but the Russian prose of *The Master and Margarita* was too dark. The devil was in Moscow with his large black cat, hosting magic shows and murdering people. I dog-eared the page, not bothering with a bookmark, and tucked the book back in my bag. But I couldn't sleep, I worried if I gave in to sleep, I'd give in to death.

My husband was not aware of this quixotic scheme in my head. He was in and out of sleep, snoring gently on the tattered brown reclining chair. Behind him, the devil's black cat perched on my hospital room's window. The cat, like in the Russian classic, was enormous, sphinxlike, and it stared back at me with glowing green eyes. The blinds were open, and the large backdrop of city lights stretched out behind it.

I turned my head away, fearful of the apparition. I looked at my husband. I didn't want to wake him. I wanted to let him rest. I'd exhausted him during the entire pregnancy, and now this.

Before I buzzed the nurse, I wanted to see if my eyes were still playing tricks on me. When I turned back to the window, the devil appeared next to the cat, wearing a cowboy hat and blazer, his legs and arms crossed. Terror drilled through me.

The devil seemed unimpressed by the city lights. Instead, he glared intensely at me, patiently waiting. I wondered if he would kill me or wait for me to die and then drag me to the Other Side while Gautam slept. Would he bring me to Laila, or would he let me burn?

I gave in to a heavy blink and turned my focus to Gautam. I had to survive. I couldn't leave the world yet. I needed to be with my husband. The characters still sat there, looking at me.

My mind grew fuzzy, and my throat clenched. I had to tell them to get out of here, to leave me alone. But I was too afraid. With the only energy I had left, I triumphantly rang the nurse's buzzer on my hospital bed. The high-pitched beeping noise woke Gautam, and he jumped up in alarm.

"Are you okay?" he asked as he rushed to my side.

"Yes, sorry to wake you. I'm having nightmares from the drugs or a fever. I already buzzed the nurse. Can you get me a glass of water?"

"You're burning up," he noted as he pressed his hands to my forehead. I gazed over at the windows again, and I no longer saw the characters from hell.

The night nurse arrived in the darkness. She gave me Motrin and ice packs to help the 104-degree fever. My father went to get ice chips for me.

"Sometimes the pain meds can cause a fever. I'll keep checking in on you," she said before she walked out of the room.

Gautam held my hand. I turned to him and whispered, "If I close my eyes, I'm afraid I will die." I clutched the hospital sheets and pulled them to my face.

"Don't think like that," he said. "I'll make sure you are safe." He stood from his chair, turned off the overhead lights, and crawled into my narrow hospital bed. I turned to my side to give him room as he held me.

"I hope so," I said, staring at the blank ceiling. I gnawed on the ice cubes and tried to think of something positive, but instead, I began to cry.

"Shh," he whispered. "You need all the rest you can get for the delivery. Try to sleep for me." He held me closer, letting me know in all the right ways that we were in this together. I sank back under the thin sheets. I wouldn't give in to sleep. I couldn't. I had to stay awake.

The morning came with soft sunlight. My parents were cuddled together on a cot, and Gautam, on the reclining chair, rustled under the thin hospital blanket. My dad checked my forehead. "Still warm," he whispered, and he went to grab me more ice chips and apple juice. I had never seen my parents so pale before. Despite all of the stitches and broken limbs they had dealt with while raising three kids, they'd never looked this disheveled. While my mother had never lost a pregnancy of her own, I couldn't imagine what it must have felt like for her to see her own baby lose a baby.

"Are you okay?" I asked her quietly, trying not to wake up Gautam.

"My tummy is upset," she said as she squirmed on the cot.

I knew how nerves could completely unsettle a stomach. I thought of the days I'd run cross-country. Before long-distance races, I'd sit in the hot porta-potty with my belly in knots.

A sharp contraction radiated through my own side. "Mine is, too, you know, since I'm in *labor*." I clutched my side, and we exchanged smirks. My dad returned and handed me the apple juice. Soon after, the nurse and a different doctor arrived.

"She's burning up," the doctor said. "Why wasn't I notified of the fever?" she asked the night nurse in a scolding tone right in front of us, even though my legs were spread and her gloved hand was inside of me, checking my cervix.

"I checked on her all night," the nurse said, casting a defensive look at the doctor. I felt bad for the nurse; she was doing a great job. She looked young, and I wondered if this was the first stillbirth she had worked. She was so determined to help us.

"She'll need antibiotics after the delivery," the doctor ordered, not cutting the nurse any slack. I was relieved that it was morning and this would all be over soon.

"I'll make sure she gets that," the nurse replied in a defeated tone.

Then the doctor noticed the wrong dose of

meds in my pain pump. Perhaps that explained why I felt like I was on my fifth cocktail and had spent the night fighting off hallucinations from *The Master and Margarita*. I also couldn't help but wonder how close I had really come to dying during the night. But none of that bothered me as much as the cramps radiating down the side of my stomach.

"I need an epidural," I said, interrupting the ongoing dialogue between the apprehensive doctor and the flustered nurse.

They brought in the anesthesiologist right away. Gautam was horrified at how I seemed to enjoy the tingling, twitching, and itchy sensation of the spinal administration; he'd always been squeamish of needles despite being a doctor's son. The numbness that ran down my legs gave me power, the power to feel nothing, and that liberated me.

After a few more hours, I was ready to deliver our daughter. The opening of my cervix felt powerful, and I think I would have found labor an intriguing exploration of new territory if my baby had been alive. My parents politely left the room, only to share with us later on that they met another pair of grandparents in the lobby whose daughter was delivering a healthy baby after a stillbirth.

"Now, push like you are having a bowel movement," the doctor instructed with a straight face.

I glanced at Gautam, and he responded with a childish smile. I was amazed that we could still smile even in the worst moment of our lives. I wanted to laugh hysterically—maybe that was from the drugs—but instead, I took awkward inhales and pushed, though I wasn't sure if it was doing anything, since I couldn't feel my legs. I felt like a dead jellyfish on the beach with children probing its loose, translucent, shimmery body.

"Almost there," the nurse cooed. I inhaled theatrically and almost felt disappointed at how easy it all felt now. Gautam gripped my hand tightly.

"And there's the baby and now the placenta," the doctor said. "It came out fast, and it's a bit small, so there might have been an infection. The cord did come out around the baby's neck, too, but all these could have been from the induced labor."

"That's it? I'm done already?" I had been watching the analog clock; the entire delivery had lasted less than ten minutes. I'd found it almost pleasurable and probably would have looked back and loved every hour of it—the sweat, the drugs, the cramping, the attention—if only the end result had brought forth life.

"You did great," the doctor said as she handed our baby to the nurse who would bathe her. "There's only a fifty percent chance you'll find out what happened. Hard to get answers, unfortunately, even with the autopsy report."

I couldn't believe that, with modern science, it was still unlikely that we'd find out the cause of death.

"What about my wife? Not too much blood

loss?" Gautam asked.

"Everything looks normal. No severe bleeding, no tearing, no need for stitches." The doctor smiled softly at me.

Relief washed over me until I realized the hardest part wasn't over yet.

"Want to hold the baby?" the nurse asked.

I gripped Gautam's hand like the world was ending. But with him by my side, a strength flowed into me. I knew I could do this. I didn't want any regrets, and I didn't want to hold Gautam back from meeting her. It was the only chance we had.

"Yes, we will see her together," I said.

You were perfect, my love. In my mind, I imagined you as an undeveloped, strange-looking, outer-space, miniature alien in my arms, but when I held you, God, all I saw was your beauty. I couldn't believe I had given birth to a child. You were wrapped in a fluffy, hand-knitted blanket with a matching hat, light pink for a girl.

You looked more like your dad. I guess the famous saying is true, that newborns look like their dads. You had a sweet little nose and little resting eyes. You weighed almost two pounds. You were pathetically perfect, as my mother said, like a little doll. Just holding you caused your left nostril to release a drop of blood. That made your father cry.

Sorry! Oh, I'm sorry for being afraid of you. I love you.

I leaned over to kiss you, but my neck was

cramped from labor, and I couldn't kiss your forehead directly. I tried to wiggle closer, but the paralysis from the epidural made me limp like roadkill. And then I sobbed.

Your dad held you the rest of the time. You looked at home in his arms. He'd have been the best dad to you. Strong, handsome, hilarious, smart. God, you would have been such a daddy's girl. I admired him.

We had a minister bless and baptize you. Even your grandparents were there to hold you and kiss you goodbye. You have a loving family, Laila.

We asked the nurse to take you away afterwards. It would be the last time I saw you. I had to be strong for everyone, especially your father. I didn't want to see him cry again. Please don't take it personally.

After you left, I felt embarrassed when I asked my mom for the memory box. She gently walked over and handed it to me as she rubbed my back. "You did great, honey," she said. I clung to the keepsake box the staff had made for me, cradling it like it was you. In my mind, it was you. The box held beautiful Polaroid pictures of your face, footprints, and handprints and your baptism certificate. It even held the clothes you wore when I held you. I'm sorry I said I didn't want the box at first. I'll never let it go.

"We'd really like you to stay another night," the doctor advised. The fever had turned into an infection. Chorioamnionitis.

"I'd like to go," I said. It was only early afternoon. Another night felt daunting.

"Your health is important," Gautam said as he stood near the doctor. "We can stay if needed." He had transformed into full caregiver mode. Around his family, he always went above and beyond to care for those who needed help, whether for his mother or grandfather.

"Fine," I said, surrendering. I felt too weak to argue as the post-labor contractions caught me by surprise, and I clenched my stomach. It felt like a cruel joke that labor pains could strike even after labor. "Can I have some medicine? The epidural wore off."

"We can give you some pain relievers. Here's a Tylenol," said the nurse. I looked at the pill, assuming she was kidding. During labor, I had been given pain medications that had made me high as a kite, but now I would only get Tylenol. I needed something stronger. Gautam handed me water to swallow the pill. It didn't make sense.

"Glad you'll stay. When you can, gather your belongings. We will move you to the recovery floor," the doctor said as she logged notes on her computer.

A recovery floor. I imagined a shared room with only a thin curtain separating me from a real mother tending to her living baby as I sobbed on the hospital bed, louder than the newborn next door.

"I can't go there. If I have to go there, I will leave," I said, my voice cracking. Not only did I want to avoid the sight of newborns, but I couldn't imagine being so far from Laila. I wanted to stay on the same floor she was on, not in a different wing. What if I wanted to see her again?

"It's an insurance issue, but let's see what we can do," the doctor said, and she signaled for the nurse to look into it.

The hospital sent a sympathy basket to our room and let us know we could remain in our room for the rest of our stay. It felt like we had won a small battle. Plus, the gesture was kind, but when I went to try the red grapes, they were rotten and covered in mold. Instead of eating the fruit, my mother and I nibbled on the chocolate chip cookies.

But my hormones screamed for me to hold our girl again. At one point, my mother had to intercept the nurse in the hallway because I had asked her to bring our baby back into the room again but had then doubted my decision. I was so concerned about upsetting Gautam again if I brought her back and thought it would be better to resist the urge instead of reopening a bleeding wound.

In another world, my daughter came back in the room with us. In another world, I knew about the various ways families spent time with their stillborn babies. I'd spent every minute with her until I had to leave. In another world, our room had a cuddle cot—a device to keep babies cool so families can hold them longer. In another world, we gave her a bath. In another world, we unwrapped her from her blanket and held her hand. In another world, we took pictures of us holding her that we could look at for years to come. In another world, we sang to her. In another world, I comforted my husband when he cried.

But I didn't know. That night, after my parents left, I had Gautam hand me Laila's memory box. I didn't open the box, but I held it like a baby in my arms. The nurse administered an oral tablet of Lorazepam when she found me, and I slept without having any dreams.

CHAPTER TEN

On the day she gave birth, everything was already taken from her. Her basic instinct to nurture was stripped down and stolen. The only thing left for her was her grief. And in her grief lived her child.

–from my notebook

My back spasmed across the thin mattress from the epidural aftermath. A nurse unhooked my arm from the fluids and antibiotics. The fever broke. Gautam groaned as he got up from the plastic chair and guided me to the bathroom. He helped me remove the off-white hospital gown and then turned on the shower and tested the water until it ran warm. The steam fogged up the mirror. A baby screeched down the hallway, which caused the hair on my neck to rise.

The shower rid me of the coated blood between my thighs. I slow-danced around the low water pressure, cupping my hands to catch the water like it was something sacred. I scrubbed the hospital soap against the gooey tape marks from the IV. Then I stared at my body, no longer feeling connected to it in any way. As I washed my flat and lifeless belly, I tried to keep the water from spreading to the epidural bandage on my back, which wasn't supposed to get wet.

I stepped out of the shower slowly, careful not to slip. Gautam dried me off with a coarse and sterile towel before opening the overnight bag. He'd been in a rush and packed the wrong size of pants, no underwear, and a sweatshirt. I reciprocated his innocent smile and made do with the mesh hospital underwear. He tried to help me with my winter coat, and it zipped up easily this time—no more baby bump for the zipper to get stuck on.

Before I left, a nurse who worked the morning shift sobbed when he hugged me. I was bothered as I patted his back to console him. He hadn't been there for the worst of it. He hadn't even seen Laila or the delivery like the other nurses, but he could so easily cry when I couldn't. I stiffened from his hug and told him, "It's okay."

Gautam guided me through the glass doors, freeing us from the hospital. Outside the confines of my hospital room, the city had changed. Ambulances rushed by with sirens screaming, such a hideous and imperfect distraction. The chaos looked beautiful, more unknown, more mysterious. The spring sun felt radiant and blinding as my eyes adapted to the light. For a moment, I felt lucky to be alive as the fresh air rushed to my face.

The death of a baby is not confined to the private

delivery room; it spreads throughout the entire labor and delivery floor. Later on, a midwife student shared with me that there's a hefty spiral notebook for the staff. After working a loss shift, an employee could sign their name below the last. I imagined the book as a black binder with a pen taped to a string for easy access. It notified others, like the sign with a raindrop on a leaf, so the staff could take turns working a loss, keeping the mental and emotional toll manageable. Maybe the pages were thick and crinkled from dried tears. I wondered how old this book was and what method had been used before. Did the staff flip a coin or play a game of rock paper scissor shoot? How did they keep finding ways to manage the fact that not all births end in life? *Rock, paper, scissors, shoot.*

As we squeezed into the back of the cab, it hit me. Our baby wasn't coming home with us. This was all wrong. The sadness made me feel as if I were melting into the worn leather seats of the cab; such loss must rank at the top of the list of worst human experiences.

"What would make you feel better?" Gautam asked once he'd helped me ease into the cab.

"Let's rescue a dog," I said. I couldn't stand the thought of an empty apartment with only the plant, Ernie, waiting for us. I craved to nurture something that needed me.

"Really?" he asked. Gautam had always wanted a dog, but his parents had forbidden it.

They'd told him how, back in India, dogs were viewed as dirty animals. His mother had even been chased by a pack of wild dogs in Kashmir.

"And let's get a drink."

"Fuck it," he said. "Let's get a dog, but the drink comes first."

Gautam froze when he walked into our apartment. One of Ernie's three stumps had been knocked over onto the floor. We'd often said that the three branches symbolized the three of us: husband, wife, and baby. Now one was tipped over and dead.

I raided the fridge for a drink. I could only find the French champagne we'd planned to pop after coming home with our baby. I held the bottle up. Gautam's expression looked pained.

"You need a proper breakfast," he said.

At the hotel restaurant down the street from our apartment, I ordered a blood orange mimosa and washed it down with the Lorazepam. Before I'd left the hospital, one of the doctors had given me a prescription. "Extenuating circumstances," he'd said, looking very pitiful. I'd gripped the pills and tucked them into my purse.

"Should you be taking that with alcohol?" Gautam asked with concern.

"I don't know, but I don't care."

Gautam flinched at my sharp tone as if I splashed water on his face. I thought of when he'd hung his head and cried while holding our daughter against his chest. My harsh words left me feeling like a villain. After all, *my* body had done this to us.

"I'm sorry," I said, softer this time.

"It's okay, but please make sure to order food, too," he said gently.

Gautam had tried to get me to eat during our time in the hospital, but my stomach had been sour. I glanced down at the menu now and ordered oatmeal, hoping the warm, bland food would help settle my stomach.

Gautam ordered a beer. As I placed my hands around the tall flute glass, my engagement ring caught the sunlight. Before, such a sight would have caused me to veer off into beautiful daydreams about my child. Now, though, I redirected my train of thought, focusing on the glistening carbonation instead. The champagne tasted bitter on my tongue, acidic with the fresh-squeezed orange juice. The taste reminded me of the first time I'd ever taken a drink in high school, how the alcohol had tasted like nail polish remover

"I'm glad you are healthy," he said.

I stroked his hand, although I didn't care much for my health; I felt guilty about my health, I should have died, if my daughter could have lived. *Save the baby or save the mother.* It dawned on me that I didn't know where the hospital stored the babies who had died, and I felt like a terrible mother since I had forgotten to ask.

My steel-cut oatmeal arrived moments later. I took a small bite and then dropped my spoon with a clatter when a woman with a black stroller passed by the window. Jealousy coursed through me, and I felt the tears start to come.

"Enjoying breakfast?" the waiter asked as he

refilled our water glasses. I nodded untruthfully. That's when I realized I would enjoy nothing about this day. Despite the strange, foreign taste of the mimosa, I ordered another because I simply had no other way to carry on.

Back home, I was still bleeding. I drew a bath to try to help me unwind. On the bathroom counter, my toiletries looked like a still life of a former existence. My cocoa butter for stretch marks sat next to my prenatal vitamins. The doctor had recommended that I continue to take prenatal vitamins to help nourish myself during the post-partum period, but I couldn't stand the idea. I swept the items into the drawer and shut it.

As I stripped down, I was stuck looking at my naked body again, and it seemed even worse with the bright lighting. My breasts were red and agitated, and a rash had spread across my spine from the epidural.

"Latex allergy," Gautam said as he gently rubbed my back. "I get that, too." He helped me rip the bandage off.

I slid off my disposable mesh underwear from the hospital and dipped my feet in first; the water was so hot that they turned red. Then I squatted over the tub and slowly lowered myself. My engorged breasts, close to three times their previous size, floated unwillingly, like ocean buoys. I traced the faint brown line extending down from my navel to my pubic hair, something I hadn't noticed before. As I followed the path down with my finger, I jumped in the tub. A thick, creamy white drop escaped from my nipple and trickled into the water like a teardrop. *Breast milk.*

The first funeral I'd ever attended was for a middle school classmate who'd lost her life from a sudden brain aneurysm. We'd shared a history class and we'd been assigned to work on an in-class activity together about Otzi the Iceman.

Side by side, we'd read through a chapter about the accidental discovery in the Alps of Europe's oldest naturally preserved mummy, and then we'd brainstormed ideas about what this discovery could mean, imagining ourselves finding the Chalcolithic remains encased in ancient ice. I cringed at the image of Otzi's shiny, leathery skin, while my classmate traced her hands around it.

At her funeral, I bravely walked up to the casket and peered in. She was wearing her pajamas, with a teddy bear tucked in her arm. I blushed at the intimate scene; it was as if someone had gently pulled her from her bed and placed her in the casket. She didn't look dead, only frozen in time.

When I'd held my daughter, I couldn't believe she was dead. She was my baby, my sleeping baby. Yes, she was smaller than most babies, but she was so beautiful and peaceful. She was undoubtedly not dead. The doctors had it all wrong. *Do all parents go through this denial when they lose a child?*

Gautam was with me when I found a spot in my closet to tuck away the memory box. Before we put it away, we opened it together to see what was inside. The sight of her hospital bracelets and polaroid photos caused him to buckle over and cry. She didn't look as I remembered her, her skin was bluer in the picture.

After that, I hid the memory box from him to protect him from the pain. Other things were hidden in my closet, too, like the newborn clothes with tags on, now used as a handkerchief to wash away tears.

A now-canceled baby shower had been planned for the upcoming weekend. I found the notification while going through my inbox, and it reminded me of how wrong everything was. I was supposed to have my shower and my baby.

A relative had ordered a pink wooden bassinet from the registry, and it arrived at our door only to be sent back immediately. When my mother and I drove the bassinet back to the store, they were unable to process a return. The original purchaser had to return the item, I couldn't.

"But the person who shipped me the gift lives in D.C," I added.

"Sorry, there's nothing we can do," the customer service representative replied in a firm voice. I knew I lost the battle, and my mother grasped my hand.

I wondered what I would have done if I'd already had the baby shower. How could I have possibly shipped back all of those items? My mother was enraged at the return policy, and deleted my registry at the store. Hours of work spent researching the perfect products for Laila disappeared without a trace.

I had insomnia, so I took an occasional Lorazepam. The hospital doctor could only prescribe me five; to get more, I would have to see a psychiatrist. I saved the drug for the nights I really couldn't close my eyes. The remaining nights, I relied on wine and Benadryl. After enough drinks, my taste buds adjusted to alcohol very well. My medications from the hospital discharge- anxiety pills, multivitamins, and antibiotics- didn't mix well with alcohol, but still, I drank. Just one more glass, just another one. Why not finish the bottle?

I think this was why I was so hesitant to hold Laila: I already knew that the particular moment of holding her, seeing her, being with her would keep me up at night in the days, weeks, months, and maybe even years to follow.

If I did manage to sleep, I woke up from dreams about holding Laila again, and my nipples leaked through my pajama blouse. In one dream, I was coming back from a trip and unpacking my suitcase. At the bottom of the bag, beneath sweatshirts and tops, I found my baby face down with her arm sticking out. Her arm was cracked, and blood, now dried, had pooled in the crook of her elbow. I pried her gently from the bag, hoping she was alive.

When I flipped her over, she wasn't breathing,

so I started doing CPR on her. I had been a summer lifeguard during high school, and I remembered how to do chest compressions on a baby. I did this for several minutes until she took a breath and smiled.

Sometimes, after these dreams, I'd wake up thinking she was alive on my chest. My heart overflowed with excitement and love. Once, I opened my eyes and saw her floating above me. When I reached for her, she vanished into the air.

I made a bold choice to go outside and get some fresh air. I walked down the block to the Australian-inspired coffee shop. Inside, the chalk-white walls and overflowing bakery products calmed me. I hadn't felt hunger for days, but I ordered a hot mocha cappuccino from the over-friendly barista.

By the time I made it home, I had broken out in hives and felt as if my chest were closing in. Gautam rushed me to the hospital. The doctor, unimpressed by my reaction, explained that "grief can cause physical reactions."

"Even chest pain?" I asked, unconvinced as I lay stiff in the hospital bed.

"Yes, grief induces somatic symptoms," he replied with a sympathetic stare. Still, he administered a low-dose allergy medication. Lochia congregated between my thighs, and a nurse brought me an ice pack to help with the breast pain. My body was falling apart.

When the doctor asked what I'd eaten that

day, I confessed that I'd only had the coffee. I still had no desire to eat. Gautam called the coffee shop, but nothing in the coffee, he learned, should have caused an anaphylactic reaction. *It was only coffee.*

I was certain I would die without my baby, that it was impossible to live. I started to see a ghostly woman behind my eyes when I was about to fall asleep. She wasn't a dream, more like a premonition. She wore a long white dress and rocked my baby in the same rocking chair I had been rocked in when I was a child. "Who are you?" I asked. She shook her head and pointed at me. "This will be you soon," she told me.

I trembled on my way to the OB-GYN for my postpartum visit. In the waiting room, eager and expecting mothers sat near me. A woman had her newborn in a car seat, and it was like she was parading around the office with a trophy. I felt like a reject; my pregnancy was the one percent that failed after twenty weeks.

In the examination room, the doctor didn't need to conduct a pelvic exam. I was disappointed. I wanted the standard protocol and to be treated like everyone else who had just delivered a child.

"When should I head back to work?" I asked the doctor.

"It depends. Some patients take up to eight weeks off. Others return after three weeks."

I thought it would make my grief less painful if I went back as soon as possible, so I decided to take the minimum time off, three weeks.

Relatives speculated that the trip to Sedona had caused the tragedy, saying that we shouldn't have traveled, that the plane ride could have caused a clotting issue, that our walks around the parks must have been too strenuous, or our kayak ride along Lake Powell could have caused some problem. Most importantly, I was warned to be more careful next time.

Their words stung, even though the trip had been approved by my obstetrician and none of these assumptions rang true to my medical staff. My stillbirth remained unexplained, a glitch, an unforeseeable tragedy that no one could control, like many others. Couples take babymoons all the time. I have told these relatives exactly what my doctor told me. Nevertheless, people don't like to hear that babies can die for no reason.

When Laila died, my world stopped. A void was created when the possibility of her life died. The halt of the momentum. The stillness. The empty space. We had no deadlines now, no long checklist of tasks to do before the baby arrived, no need to buy a car or move to a larger apartment. Now we stayed still.

After only a week, family members wanted to "see" or "hear" that I was back at work. Some even suggested I return earlier than three weeks so I wasn't sitting at home doing nothing all day, as if grieving wasn't the proper way to be spending my time. I got very defensive and angry that my time to heal had become everyone else's choice except mine.

Throughout the pregnancy, not once did I imagine myself with my baby. I could see myself using the latest tools on the registry, like the LED night-vision camera that connects to an app on your phone. I could imagine the new high-rise condo we would live in. I could see future arguments with Gautam because I was lazy and tired. I could see my mother coming over to help babysit.

Not once, though, did I see myself or dream about changing Laila's clothes, holding her hands, kissing her face, nursing her, or rocking her. I didn't see anything like that. I chalked it up to being focused on the present and checking off the endless to-do list to get ready for the baby. I was busy navigating the world as a young pregnant person, tuning out every older person's tacky advice about child-rearing. I had so much chatter going into my ear that I didn't have time to collect my thoughts. I didn't have time to think. It hadn't hit me yet that I was going to be a mother.

People say that the third trimester is when it really hits you. Right before my third trimester, it really hit me. I felt like I'd never get the chance to know what preparing for motherhood is like. I was left with a yearning for what could have been, what it would have been like to rock her, to hold her, and a regret that I never let myself focus on imagining her more before she left me.

I watched movies. I forget what kind. Maybe horror movies. A few friends visited and dropped off food, although I wasn't eating much. Retelling events seemed like a waste of time; it wouldn't bring Laila back. I kept the details minimal. I kept my suicidal thoughts to myself, the images flashing before me of my death, which would lead me back to my daughter.

Some friend tried to cheer me up by noting how my body had already "bounced back." The postpartum weight-loss trend seemed incredibly silly to me. I wondered why mothers cared so much about weight when they had a living and breathing baby in their arms. I joked to one friend that nothing gets rid of an appetite like grief.

Sometimes my body made up for my lack of slumber by sending me into a dark cave of REM. I wasn't sure if my dreams were nightmares, because sometimes I was so happy to see Laila, even though she was still dead. My throat became warm, and my chest buzzed, as though saying, "This is love. This is real love."

She would giggle as she opened her brown eyes wide. In my dreams, her image was on Polaroids, stacks and stacks of them. I looked through them all, clutching them, unable to pick my favorite.

They felt like proof that she was alive and happy in another world.

My mother dreamed of Laila, too. She dreamed of a nurse dressed in white, taking care of my baby in a heavenly NICU. *I told you, baby. She's safe, and she'll come back to you.* My mother dreamed that she was with Hilda, asking her how the afterlife was. Then she snuck away with Laila in her arms, trying to escape and bring her back to earth. When she woke up, Laila was gone.

In our dreams, we were without pain and intoxicated by Laila's life. For a moment, we were blessed because our worry lifted and her granddaughter, my daughter, was present and whole.

I needed something to live for. Sleep was pointless. My breasts throbbed without ice. I crept into the kitchen and grabbed a bag of frozen peas from the freezer, careful not to wake Gautam.

On the couch, I propped my laptop open and scrolled through the local animal shelter's website. I landed on the face of a mixed lab-retriever breed with large, round eyes. Dog name: Leigh. Age: four months. Gender: female. Housetrained: unknown. *That's the one*, I thought. I saved the number of the shelter in my phone and noted their hours of operation. I'd call as soon as they opened.

CHAPTER ELEVEN

The few days we waited to hear from the shelter blurred together without sleep. That dog was the only one I wanted. There were no others. I'd provided the shelter a list of references and even noted that we lived right in front of Rittenhouse Park to make up for the fact we had a one-bed-room apartment.

When we finally were cleared to pick the dog up, I bundled up in the only clothes that fit me, a pair of forest-green sweatpants and a discounted puffer jacket I'd bought before our trip to Iceland. I had already boxed up my maternity clothes; they were far too triggering to wear or to even see in my closet. The Iceland trip seemed like a foggy memory from the past, a time when life and love had been simple and easy. I knew I'd never be happy like that again.

"What should we name her?" Gautam asked as he held my hand. The dog's original name, Leigh, was too much like my own.

"I like Disney names," I admitted, feeling childish. A weight lifted off us, even if just for a moment, and we felt excited about something as a couple again.

I then felt very sad, as I recalled when the hospital staff had asked us for our baby's name. I had been too embarrassed to give Laila her middle name, Paris, so she was only Laila. Not for her birth certificate, but for her fetal death certificate. It had felt like a cruel joke.

How can someone be given a death certificate but not a birth certificate first? A few years later, I learned that Pennsylvania was one of the states to offer stillbirth birth certificates for bereaved parents. I printed and mailed out Laila's information immediately, but her records could not be located to produce a certificate, and my calls to the state went unanswered.

"How about Cinderella?" Gautam asked, and my face stiffened in a smile. I could imagine a fluffy and small pure-bred dog having such a name, but a black lab mix?

Cinderella, it was—Ella for short—because it made me laugh for the first time since our baby had died.

Inside the store, I flung my arms around the tailless puppy. Rescued from Kentucky, she'd been the only puppy in her litter to survive. I controlled my tears and desire to gush my entire story of the past few days to the store clerk, certain that if I did, she'd rescind my application in big, bold red letters—dogs aren't safe around grief-stricken mothers who lost their babies only days ago.

The dog was receptive to my hug, and she let me hold her warm body close to mine before quickly dashing out of her crate to nuzzle her face into the nearby toy bin. Gautam and I laughed and went overboard with purchases: puppy food, teething toys, a crate, a leash, a harness. She had everything she needed. She didn't know how to walk on a leash and cowered when we brought her outside into the booming city.

As soon as Gautam lifted her into his arms, a splash of color returned to his face.

"Time to take you home," he whispered into the dog's bat-like ear.

I had a naïve idea that the puppy would be immediately good and obedient, like dogs in the movies nurturing their sick owner. I felt dead inside, after all. I'd never had a dog before, but I knew animals could sense when people were ill, and I thought the puppy would want to snuggle and tend to my broken heart.

She was good for the first day or so, quietly adapting to her new surroundings while I was on my self-declared bedrest. But as soon as she felt comfortable, her wild puppy personality emerged. Hyper and relentless, she tried to nudge me off the couch, coaxing me to play with all of her new toys. She had accidents and nibbled through my sweatpants with her razor-sharp teeth. She'd need to go out more than ten times a day.

In an apartment building, her demands felt even more strenuous. I longed for a home with a backyard, where I could simply open a screen door to let her out. I often carried her down the hallway to the elevator when she refused to walk on the leash, although my back still ached from the epidural.

One day, my back hurt too much, but when I put her on the ground to walk out of our apartment, she refused to move.

"Please be good for your mommy," I begged as I tugged lightly on the leash.

She clenched her jaws around the leash, wanting to play tug of war.

"This was a mistake. I want my child back. I want my daughter back," I said as I dropped the leash. She gazed at me with her gooey black eyes and shrank back with her ears glued to her head. I wrapped my arms around her and cried into her fur.

Although she couldn't possibly understand, her round eyes were still forgiving. I picked her up and carried her all the way down the hallway.

When I held Laila's memorial box and clutched the little dress she would have worn for her newborn photo session, I thought about death. The dress was pink and had a sequined star in the center and an attached pink tutu. I'd wondered when I'd bought it if it would be too itchy for her sensitive newborn skin, but she'd only have worn it for a few professional pictures. Now, as I held this dress, I wanted death. Death had taken her from me, but it was also the only door back to her. I wanted death to take me to my daughter.

I wanted pure death, not reincarnation. I didn't like the idea that my daughter could come back as something other than what she was. My baby. I wanted my daughter to be a person, her and no one else. That's why I thought my best shot was death, face to face.

I knew there was no guarantee that would actually happen, that it could be just a fantasy and not the reality when we die. *Is there still a reality when we die?* I needed to see her again.

At first, we had agreed to let the hospital do the arrangements for a funeral, but then we decided we wanted her ashes. I shuffled through discharge paperwork and realized that I needed to contact the funeral parlor. The social worker had highlighted the number for me on the grief pamphlet, as if she'd known I'd need it to be accessible.

"Let me check the records to see if she has been picked up yet," the staff member at the parlor said when I called.

"What do you mean? It has been over a week," I replied as I hunched over on the corner of my bed.

"The staff makes monthly visits to collect the babies."

"Oh." I felt sick to my stomach at the idea of Laila being alone at the hospital long after we left. She could still be there, and the thought caused me to tremble. *The death of one baby doesn't warrant an immediate pick-up.*

"I checked. We do have her, and we can make those arrangements. It'll be three hundred dollars."

"OK. Thanks," I said as I exhaled, glad she wasn't still there. It was strange to reduce her body to a transaction, and I was haunted at the thought that I had almost missed out on getting her ashes. If I hadn't called, she would have been by the church in the baby section of Laurel Hill Cemetery. I had no clue where that cemetery was located.

I collapsed onto the kitchen floor when I sensed the moment she burned. My skin was on fire. I whispered, "I'm so sorry, baby." I then wondered if I should have instead paid for a proper burial at my family's lot; she could have rested next to my great-grandmother's daughter. My mother said that would have cost ten thousand dollars, but I still wondered if it would have been worth it. Had I made the wrong decision? Terrible thoughts haunted me: *What if her soul was still in her body and she felt pain when she was cremated?*

A late spring snowstorm made the city quiet. I woke up at six in the morning to take Ella out to the park. She was growing into her body more and walked better on the leash as long as I had a pocket full of training treats to give her as a reward. Outside, the park was covered in a pure white blanket of fresh snow. No one else was out yet; no footprints broke the landscape. Ella's little nub of a tail wiggled rapidly as we walked closer to the field.

I extended Ella's retractable leash to let her prance through the snow. As her thick fur caught white flakes, she chomped like an alligator at the snowflakes falling from the sky. An unfamiliar sensation of joy crept across my heavy chest. I didn't think I'd ever feel happiness again.

Back inside, the snow melted on us, making us damp.

"A baby and now a puppy?" a neighbor exclaimed when he held the elevator door open for me. He was already dressed in a suit. Ella panted near my feet.

"Oh. No baby. She passed away," I replied, and the elevator doors shut quickly behind us.

Gautam was squeamish with needles, so he didn't come with me to my tattoo appointment. I didn't mind that he wasn't there. Sometimes, my grief felt personal, as if it were only mine, and I had to do my own things to heal, like getting a tattoo for the first time. I wanted it in a visible spot, my shoulder, before I returned to work. I wanted a piece of Laila with me as proof that she had been here, that she had lived, that she had come to Earth, if only for a fleeting moment.

I brought Laila's original hospital ink hand-prints to the tattoo parlor. I was mortified when the tattoo artist put the memorial item into the scanner and paranoid that the image would smear.

When he handed it back to me, I was relieved. The paper was fine; her hand and footprints didn't smear. With the scanned copy, he went into a communal wooden table and began to trace the images.

"Do you like this?" he asked as he held up a sketched outline of her handprints. The pencil sketch looked like nothing like her handprints, but I said yes anyway. I trusted that he knew what he was doing. He led me back to his rented room. His artwork lined the walls.

He applied rubbing alcohol to my shoulder and began. The needle didn't hurt.

"How old is your baby?" he asked.

"She passed away a few weeks ago; it's a memorial tattoo."

"I'm sorry." For the rest of the session, he remained silent, processing and focusing on the needle. I longed for a conversation. Surely, tattoo artists have their own personal battles, but if he did, he kept them to himself.

He showed me the image in the mirror. The handprints were identical.

"Thanks for bringing my baby back." I gave him a large tip.

He laced a bandage over the tattoo. "This will need to stay dry for a few hours."

When I left the tattoo parlor, it began to rain. The wind carried the smell of warmth, which was finally coming to the area after winter's extended stay. I hid my body, clinging to my rain jacket, as I didn't want anything to happen to her hand-prints. Even the scanned copy the tattoo artist had made was important to me.

After a few hours, I was allowed to take off the bandage. I kept the care instructions by the bath-room sink, reminding myself of the tasks I had to do, like not to submerge the tattoo in water, to keep it out of direct sunlight, and to clean the area with an antiseptic soap. That night, I wanted to join Gautam in the shower, so he could help me keep my shoulder dry as I did a quick rinse of my body. We used to shower together back when we'd first started dating and been obsessed with our naked bodies close to each other.

"Can I come in?" I asked over the rushing water.

Gautam popped his head out of the shower. He drew back the curtain and helped me inside. Then he gently took the bandage off my shoulder, careful not to hurt my skin.

"Wait a minute," he said with both hands on my shoulder. I was shivering at this point and wanted to stand beneath the warm water.

"Well, what?" I snapped. "I can't get my shoulder wet," I reminded him.

Grief made me short-tempered, easily provoked at times, but as usual, he remained patient.

"I know. I was trying to see whose hands hers look like."

I peered over and caught him comparing his palm to her handprints on my shoulder, and the thought melted me.

In my dream, I saw Laila. I was at a museum. I begged the security guard to let me in, although I didn't have a ticket. He did.

I ran to the first display. It held a picture of my tattoo of Laila's handprints on my shoulder, and the infant-loss memorial ribbon was tucked in between. And then Laila appeared.

She was on display, perched against a doll stand from my childhood, where my mother would display a porcelain doll. I only had two such dolls; one was from a birthday, and the other my baptism. Laila was dressed in white, as if she'd just had a baptism of her own. She looked angelic with her warm brown eyes.

I held her close to my chest and felt a warm, purring sensation spread across my chest. I had her. I ran out of the building with her, only to wake up without her, but the feeling in my chest lingered for a few blissful seconds.

This is what it feels like to hold your baby.

And it was only a dream.

I had a dream I was at a museum again. This time, no bodyguards stopped me from entering a closed-off section. I was glad my subconscious had ruled out the bodyguards as unnecessary characters. This time around, I was free to wander through the gallery. I passed a display of my favorite writer, Sylvia Plath. This standing closet held outfits that Plath used to wear. I rifled through the long, pale dresses, although I would have had no idea what she wore. I watched a little girl try on one of Plath's outfits. There was a sad autobiographical note about her life and how she had taken her life with her children in the house. I felt a little angry about that. How could someone leave their kids behind?

After I passed her stand, I came to my own.

My section had two poster-size images of Laila. Another was of a baby that I didn't know, but he was wearing all blue. Neither baby had their eyes open.

Will I have another stillborn?

We signed our dog up for a training class. One of the perks of having a hyper dog was that she was an excellent dog for training. I learned a lot about appropriately rewarding a dog, and she passed her beginner courses with flying colors.

Our dog trainer was a thin lady from West Philly. She lived with two greyhounds in her apartment and adored Ella. She said that if Ella weren't a puppy, she would steal her from us. We opted for additional private lessons since Ella loved the training. She learned directions like when to turn left and right and even how to jump through a hula hoop.

One day, as I walked through the pet store with the trainer, she taught me how to do a recall command with Ella. Ella was at the end of the food aisle, and once I said, "Touch," she stormed down the aisle and put her snout in my palm.

As the trainer handed Ella a handful of bite-sized jerky, she noticed my fresh ink and asked, "Aw, I didn't know you had a baby, too! How old?"

"It's a memorial tattoo."

"I'm sorry." The trainer lost her breath for a moment, and her eyes dropped. "How far along were you?"

"Seven months."

"I also lost a baby around that time, too."

We stood there alone in the dog kibble aisle like wounded soldiers. She was the first person I'd met who'd had a similar experience.

Soon strangers were complimenting Gautam and me on what a well-behaved puppy we had. The big secret with dog training was that a good dog was dependent on the owner. I had to change my approach, and I learned how to be better.

While I still wasn't the carefree dog owner who cooed in a high-pitched voice to the puppy, I took a different attitude with her. I cleaned up her puppy messes, fed her, bathed her, satisfying to some degree my nurturing instincts. I got stronger, she grew more obedient, and we went out for frequent walks together. She tended to me in her own way. She provided me with fresh air. Without her, I'd be rotting inside the apartment with the plant. And during the nights I cried, holding my daughter's memory box, she'd leap onto the bed to pound my face with kisses and nibble my neck. Sometimes she'd quietly ball up against my foot or rest her head on my thigh, and I'd dig my fingers into her coarse black fur.

CHAPTER TWELVE

On my first day back at work, I was still bleeding. My large maxi-pads felt like overfilled sponges and gave me rashes. My body didn't fit into my pre-pregnancy clothes; my cotton midi-dresses were the only things that fit. I made sure to wear a dress with a low neckline to reveal Laila's handprints and show my coworkers I was still a mother.

My thighs were pale from lack of sunlight and twice their average size, full of fatty white cellulite. I had gone from being a glowing pregnant girl to a barren one. My dresses were too short because of my weight. My face had lost its glow. My large breasts sagged. My hips were too wide. I walked around the office, embarrassed and exposed. I took the back door to bypass the bullpen of men whenever I had to use the restroom.

At first, my proximity to the kitchenette was nice. The friendly office chatter while employees grabbed their coffee offered a nice distraction. Some coworkers, the ones I wouldn't expect, even hugged me when they saw me and shared their condolences.

My throat was dry, but the water cooler was empty. I went to replace the jug, but a financial advisor stopped me as I reached for it.

"You should probably wait a few more months before trying to lift something like that."

"Thank you," I said, and my smile was awkward and curled with delight. Someone finally recognized that I had been pregnant. Already, so many things about my pregnancy had become erased. I could no longer speak about it without scaring others. But he knew things like physical recovery time after you have kids because he and his wife had toddlers. I had an opportunity to talk with him more about it, run with the conversation, but instead, I hovered there and watched him replace the water.

I dreamed that my tattoo disappeared from my shoulder. When I went to look for Laila's name and handprint in the mirror, it vanished. I was petrified in my dream. My heart was racing, and my mouth was dry when I woke up. That morning, I received a companywide email saying that we had to conceal any tattoos.

It wasn't until later, when my coworkers talked to me about their kids, that I realized I had an invisible child. Their kids had soccer games, and I imagined Laila playing soccer like her father. Their kids had a ballet recital, and I also imagined Laila being a dancer. I wondered if they knew how their conversations were toxic and how pathetically jealous I felt of everyone. Why did my child have to be invisible? Why did her life have to be a hushed topic?

One afternoon, a coworker wore his headset while chatting to a client and microwaving his coffee. He boasted about how his wife wanted to try again for another child. I felt bitter and infuriated that he would talk so loudly about future babies when I was nearby, like trying again was a joyful and easy thing to do, like everyone had this luxury that I didn't. I was infuriated.

I was flagged for being hostile in emails. I burned through PTO days. The world was against me. I couldn't even work on easy projects. When my employer suggested that I needed more time and should apply for short-term leave for the summer, I cried even though others could see me through the glass windows of the conference room.

I came home from work with blotchy skin from the tears. I had failed. I ran to Laila's keepsake box and sobbed. The daydreams of dying came back, controlling and clouding my vision. The small whispers continued: *Die, die, die to be back with your girl. Just die.*

The lady on the suicide hotline was very kind. I explained to her that my transition back to work had been terrible. She listened patiently as I said my family had hoped that returning to work would make me feel better. I'd hoped that, too, and since I was struggling so much at work, I felt like a failure all over again. I also told her about the blame I imagined others felt towards me for losing the baby, and even worse, my own self-blame. My doctors had tried to tell me that I had done nothing wrong, that gestational death can occur for no reason. Everyone seemed to think I should work through my grief, but since I couldn't seem to manage to do that, how was I supposed to survive this loss? My own body had been incapable of sustaining my baby's life, and now it seemed incapable of sustaining mine.

"Are you alone, dear?" the woman asked.

"My dog is here with me, and my husband will be home soon."

"Then let me stay on the line with you until your husband gets there."

"Thank you."

For a while, we talked about the companionship our animals bring to us. I kept petting Ella as the counselor told me about her cat, gave me resources for local support groups, and asked if I had a therapist.

"Yes, and I can start therapy again," I replied.

When Gautam returned, Ella was still kissing the tears from my face. I told him everything.

"Please call me if this happens again," he said, and his arms went around me. My sadness felt too great for the two of us. I felt that my grief would kill our relationship. Gautam kept his grief contained, but mine was messy and dangerous. I didn't want to drag him down with me.

"You have enough on your plate. I didn't want to upset you."

"You can't take this all on your shoulders.

And I'm glad you are getting the extra time off. We can work on ways to get you healthy."

I hadn't thought of myself as sick, but the idea of self-care over the summer seemed to comfort me. We scheduled an appointment with my therapist together. Afterward, he wanted me to go outside with him and get some fresh air. A walk was the last thing I wanted to do, but he looked hopeful.

By the time we made it to the Schuylkill River Trail, the sky was already dark. The streetlights cast a dim glow on the uneven pavement. I could see the long path from the end of Center City to the art museum at the trailhead. Suddenly I wanted to jog. I hadn't wanted to run in years, but now I wanted to try. *What is happening to me? How is this my life?*

"I want to run. I'll go to that the lamppost and back," I told Gautam. The lamppost looked about half a mile away.

"Sure, I'll be here with the dog."

As I started to jog, I was embarrassed that Gautam could see me. My thighs rubbed together, and I was far from the former collegiate runner I'd once been. I was gasping for air, and my stomach still felt tender.

The lamppost let off a calming fluorescent glow. As I drew closer to it, I sucked in air, panting, and the suicidal ideas from earlier in the day lifted for a moment. I felt a tug in my chest, similar to how I felt when I woke from dreams about Laila. Chills ran up my arm. Here's an idea: start running. The thought was like a song I hadn't heard since childhood.

I jogged the last half-mile back, and Gautam and Ella were sitting on a bench. When she saw me approaching, she gave me a big, toothy grin and jumped on me in congratulations.

"How was it?" Gautam asked as I sat down next to him on the bench. We looked out at the dark Schuylkill River. Back in the seventies, I heard it ran green with pollution. While it was better now, its mud-brown color wasn't charming.

"It was hard, but I miss running," I said, taking deep breaths and pulling up my top for a moment to wipe away my face sweat before it dripped into my eye.

"Well, why don't you start running again? The weather is getting so nice out now."

CHAPTER THIRTEEN

In high school, I made the cross-country team. The truth is, they were desperate for bodies and didn't actually make any cuts. I ran with the slowest group, one brunette and a blonde. They could talk the entire run while I panted. I was so self-conscious of my breath, but I couldn't control it. Their strides were in sync, reminding me of two flying geese.

Another runner joined our slow group, Amanda. When her long black hair was tied back, her stark, pale skin and deep blue eyes resembled those of a movie star. She was new to the neighborhood and, like me, didn't have any friends. I had no excuse, though, besides being freakishly quiet. After enough runs, our strides became in sync like the others, and we turned into a pair of our own.

Once, after practice, we walked the mile back home together instead of taking the bus, cutting down the trail behind the high school where kids would smoke or make out.

Instead of the usual, pretending like we had something better to do than hang out after school. I paused. "Would you want to come over sometime?"

And that sealed our friendship.

When there wasn't practice, we would run together. An elementary school was exactly half a mile away from our homes, and we warmed up our stiff muscles by running to the school and stretching before beginning our real run. We'd run to neighboring towns, through the wealthy neighborhoods, and dream about our future success. We'd scrounge together money to stop for breaks at coffee shops or for lunch, and we'd split whatever we bought. We ran as far as we could go. Even when her toenails fell off and my shoes got holes in them, we kept going, as running gave us the independence we sought.

On our first race day, she saved a seat next to me on the bus. We were curled up so close to one another that our kneecaps touched, and we shared headphones as we listened to pump-up music on her iPod. Our favorite artist was MIA. That became our routine, and after that, we were inseparable.

We had our first friend break-up over loving the same guy. He chose her over me. I had no one to sit with at lunch for weeks, so I faked an illness and sat in the nurse's office instead. She quit the team, but I still ran.

To fill the absence, I became obsessed with getting faster. It would fix all my problems. If I ran fast enough, I could get a scholarship to run somewhere in college, a guaranteed escape, somewhere far away. I trained. I read running books for inspiration, tales about Division One and ultra-marathon runners who ate grainy food and ran barefoot. I cried as I watched a documentary about Steve Prefontaine. I was obsessed with Olympian Kara Goucher. I cut her headshots out of *Runner's World* magazine and taped them onto my white chipped bookshelf like it was a junky shrine. Each season, I got faster. By the time I was a senior, I was awarded the MVP on my team.

I trained with the men's distance team to get faster, but I never was fast enough. In the end, I was defeated and picked a liberal arts college that was smaller than my high school. It wasn't Division One or Two, but there was a Division Three track team. The coach liked me. I felt wanted, a sense of belonging that I never had in high school. I was going to be an athlete—a varsity runner.

The preseason started a few weeks before classes began. There were two freshmen dormitories, and one was famous because J.D. Salinger had stayed there before dropping out after one semester. I visualized him sitting in his old dorm, smoking cigarettes, getting inspired to write *The Catcher and the Rye*, driven by his hatred of trivial Pennsylvanian towns. I lived in the other dorm.

My single room, with its thin, pale-yellow walls, smelled like burnt coffee and stale cigarettes. My parents helped me settle in to the top floor, the honors floor. It was a quiet hall with only single dorm rooms. I didn't want a roommate. My dad snuck a glance at one of the guys living on the floor.

"I didn't realize it was co-ed," he said, sensing danger.

I shrugged.

He carried a window unit air conditioner up all the stairs while my mother filed away non-perishable snacks in a plastic container beneath my bed.

I ended up being popular at college. On Friday nights, the girls on the team would flock to my single dorm room, and I'd pile make-up on their faces and do their hair. There wasn't much to do on the weekends except drink at the fraternity flats.

I wondered when they would forget about me and toss me aside for something shinier.

Although I trained harder than ever, I never met the expectations I set for myself. I lost myself behind the faster runners as we ran through farmland and cornfields and deep in the woods.

Summer training was lonely, away from my team of girls who kept me going through freshman year. In the mornings, I ran down a long strip of highway stretching from my middle-class development to the mansions. That summer, I'd commute into the city for an office job. On the commuter rail, women held copies of *Fifty Shades of Grey* to their noses. I was embarrassed if someone caught me reading it, so I read mine on my tablet, a gift I'd received when I'd graduated from high school. Everyone thought the book was romantic, and so did I. I wanted a relationship like that, a love that scared me. A love that hurt. A love that turned you on from the pain. I got my wish.

He was old enough to need reading glasses, and he wrote me love letters from the Southwest. He was rich compared to college guys and sophisticated. He gifted me books with inscriptions and treated me like a woman, not a girl. I was served my first glass of wine with him at a bar and fell in love for the first time.

Our relationship was like having a snake constrict around my chest. I couldn't escape his grasp. When I finally ended things, he turned violent.

It was spring, and the morning after I broke up with him, I tried to run. I had already quit cross-country by then, and I was barely staying afloat in my academics. The sun was still low when I found myself miles down the Perkiomen Trail, and I stopped where the grass was high and clutched my pelvis, feeling sharp needles. I was damp between my legs, not because of sweat but because of what he had done.

I went to the campus nurse as soon as it opened. She examined me and said, "Just some muscular trauma. It looks terrible, but it will heal. Did you have rough sex?"

Rough sex, yes. So rough that he pinned me down on my cheap springy mattress even after I told him to stop. So rough that he continued even when I said he was hurting me. But he was mad about the break-up. His dark eyes turned black and narrowed to slits. He kept going. His member became a weapon, tearing skin that wasn't meant to be penetrated. I was the one who wanted it, after all. He sped off in a rage in his car. I never heard from him again.

After that, I stopped running. Unlike other running injuries, like stress fractures or sprained ankles, the depth of this hurt was physical and emotional. I swore to myself I'd never be a runner again and I'd never fall in love.

Back then, I did the only thing I could do: I dropped out of college and moved back home. The girls on my team forgot about me. One even said, "It was like you fell off the face of the earth." I couldn't blame them; they had no clue. I wouldn't tell anyone, staying silent for ten years.

Amanda was there when I came back home. At the time, she'd also dropped out of college. She got a kick out of being an art school dropout; she thought it was so funny that she wanted to design a shirt that stated it.

She lived with the same boyfriend who had ended our friendship years ago. It all seemed silly now. She nurtured me when I healed from that relationship. I was diagnosed with panic disorder and agoraphobia in therapy, but I didn't tell her why. I could scarcely leave my house, but like old times, she got me outside of the house and we walked throughout the neighborhood.

In the end, we fought again when I was healthy enough to re-enroll in college and she didn't. Maybe if I had told her what had happened to me, she would have understood why I pushed her away. This was before she became a full-time yoga teacher and bartender. This was before she met and fell in love with the man she married the same year I married Gautam at the same courthouse. This was before she tragically died at twenty-six in a motorcycle accident—she was a passenger when it crashed while making a sharp turn on a dark and rainy night. Sometimes I imagine Amanda taking care of Laila on the Other Side.

But that man, the one I used to be afraid of when I ran, was now powerless, far away in the past. I thought of my one-mile run on the river trail. I thought of my daughter, and it was like she had given me the gift of fearlessness. I could run as a way to heal.

In the evenings, we continued the routine. Gautam and I would head down to the water, and he would walk with the dog and take her to the dog park while I snuck in a quick jog. The run would interrupt my thoughts of dying.

It wasn't much, but something about being outside and feeling the warm breeze made me feel a little closer to freedom.

CHAPTER FOURTEEN

I signed up for a local 5k on a whim. I hadn't raced since college, but I felt confident I could run three miles. A race would give me more motivation than running on my own. This one had been scheduled at my alma matter in memory of a college student who had died years ago. Gautam and Ella walked with me to the start line. When the gun fired, I took off.

I looped through the residential streets of University City, passing through areas I had frequented as an undergrad: the local bars, a convenience store, and a few fraternity houses. My breathing turned shallow after only a few minutes into the run, while, nearby, two college-aged girls ran side by side at a conversational pace. This was easy for them. I pushed myself to keep up with them and felt my face get hot. I wondered when I'd get back in shape and be able to talk when I ran.

When I finished the race, Ella jumped onto me and licked my salty face. Gautam handed me a bottle of water. I'd run at an 8:30-mile pace, which turned out to be a twenty-six-minute 5k. Not bad.

The adrenaline rush from the race carried me over until the next one. Each weekend, I ran all sorts of charity races, for premature babies, breast cancer, endangered rhinos, bereavement centers, veterans, and local high schools. I had so many complementary race shirts in my dresser.

As Mother's Day approached, I craved something longer than a 5k, so I registered for a 15.5-mile/ 25k trail race to distract me. I'd never run that distance, not even in college, and I was intrigued by how impossible it seemed. I wanted to do it.

However, I hadn't trained nearly enough in the past few weeks to run this race. In fact, I had barely hit a total of thirty miles. My log consisted of one- to three-mile runs, some yoga, and weight-lifting. I had done one six-mile run, and I felt like that was the maximum amount I could do.

But when I saw pictures of the scenic trail and the rolling green hills tucked away in the woods, on impulse, I registered for the race. I craved the wilderness. *I've lost my mind*, I told myself. *There's no way.* Gautam was worried about me and thought it was as wild as I did. I was so scared that I would hurt myself, and I almost let the fear talk me out of it. But then I decided I would run for Laila.

To my therapist, I admitted how I had dreamed about death because I thought I would see my baby again. I was certain I would be flagged as suicidal and taken away. To suggest that I had things under control, I told her how running helped me feel better.

With a consoling expression, she replied, "That's a normal response to grief." Then she asked if there was anything else, if I'd had thoughts of self-harm or a plan to harm myself. I did not.

However, I kept back one piece of information. I still saw that ghostly woman from time to time, the one who rocked my baby, told me I would die soon, and said that, in an alternate world, I was already dead and with my child. I didn't want to push my luck. I said nothing else. I wouldn't tell anyone about that vision.

The shoes I usually ran in wouldn't have enough traction for a trail race. The course was ranked as technical, which, from the race's reviews, I learned meant hard, uphill, roots, and lots of stuff to trip on. The slippery rubber soles of my regular shoes wouldn't help much. I needed trail shoes.

I went to a running store around the corner. I was self-conscious when the salesperson helped me try on a pair of new trail shoes and laced them up for me. I was heavier and didn't feel like a runner. Plus, I was wearing capris, and I'd forgotten to shave.

I hurriedly bought the shoes without testing out the other models. As I was walked over the counter to check out, a familiar face greeted me at the register.

"Great to see you still run!" the excitable cashier said.

I had trouble placing her at first, and then I realized we had gone to high school together. She was a few years younger than me, and we'd run track together.

"This is deceiving. I'm just getting back into shape. It's been close to five years since I ran," I admitted.

"Didn't you run cross-country in college?" she asked as she scanned the shoes.

"For a little, before I transferred colleges. How about you?"

"I actually ran my first marathon last year," she replied as she put the shoes into the bag.

"Well, my 25k trail race tomorrow feels so inadequate now!"

"Don't say that! You'll do great," she said with a smile. I still couldn't remember her name.

When I left the store, I felt embarrassed about admitting that I'd taken such a long hiatus from running. As the captain of the track team, I'd been known for being a dedicated runner. I was worried she might look up the race results from my trail race tomorrow and see how slow I'd become.

I took a deep breath and reminded myself that my running was not about competition. Right now, it was about being healthy and healing. But there was still a small competitive voice inside my head: *You should run a marathon one day.*

It was an obscene thought, so impossible I wanted to laugh.

To compensate for my lack of training, I brought

other things to the race to make me feel more prepared, like a bright red CamelBak hydration pack and a sun visor. The trail would be marked with small pink ribbons, but the reviews said that sometimes the ribbons could get torn down, so I printed out a map of the trail and kept it in a Ziploc bag along with two red Advil.

I caught a cab out of the city to Pennypack Park in Southampton, Pennsylvania. Gautam would meet me at the finish line since the race could take hours to finish. He wasn't a morning person, and the back-to-back races I had on the weekends exhausted him. He needed his rest.

I hadn't heard of the park before, and relief flooded me as I saw hundreds of runners head through the parking lot to the wooden pavilion. I was in the right place. An accordion blasted from the speakers, playing folk music. It amazed me that the city had so much to offer. You wouldn't expect a park of this size to be so close to Center City. Runners had even traveled from New York to come to this race.

After a long wait for the porta-potty, I made it to the start line. I wore my brand-new trail shoes, which I hadn't broken in. My hydration backpack was filled to the brim. I walked to the back of the pack of runners, knowing that it'd be a miracle if I crossed the finish line.

The beginning of the course was on a tight trail with lots of elevation changes. We squeezed and bumped elbows as a group of three hundred runners crammed onto the small sand trail in the clearing in the woods. I was gassed as I tried to keep up with the back of the pack, and after forty minutes of lost footing, I didn't think I could finish. I made it to the first rest stop at mile five and drank Gatorade. My backpack was heavy, and I stopped to drain some water out. An older runner with unruly, curly brown hair who had paced with me stopped, too.

"I can't do this," I admitted to her as I tried to suck in my breath. It felt like I was breathing through a straw.

"You can. Take a layer off. That long-sleeve might be causing you to overheat."

I nodded and thanked her, and as she continued on her way, I took off my long performance shirt and tied it around my waist. Then, after taking a moment to catch my breath and cool off, I pushed aside my desire to stop and kept going.

By mile eight, my legs met pavement and lavished in the ease of the road, so much more forgiving than the hard and technical trail. As I ran, I conversed with a few older runners, who stayed with me until the end of the race.

At mile twelve was the famous windy bend, where the presence of Laila overcame me, and I knew I was close to the end. After the bend was a straight mulch path, where I passed a pregnant woman with a short bob and muscular thighs in spandex. She got held up crawling over a fallen tree stump on the course, while I hopped up and over the log. She looked far into her third trimester, and the old me would have thought the due date was close. It was May. Laila had been due at the beginning of June.

I didn't like pregnant women anymore. While I used to feel a sense of camaraderie, now they only caused me distress. I was jealous, envious, and terrified of them all at the same time. Even worse, I was annoyed that she had been faster than me for most of the race. She'd even beaten me at that.

My husband saw her cross the line and shook his head with disapproval. I was proud that he felt the same way. The old me would have supported a woman doing such an admirable thing with her body; the new me wanted to tell her to do everything she could to keep her baby safe. *What if her baby overheats? What if she tripped on the technical course and fell? What if she dehydrates?*

Afterward, the craving to run a longer race entered my mind. If I could jog close to sixteen miles without training, I bet I could do a marathon if I trained. But I dismissed the thought.

CHAPTER FIFTEEN

On Memorial Day weekend, the pool in our apartment complex opened. I realized that this could be a way to get through my entire summer off. A drink could take the edge off, arguably better than running ever could. With the extra pounds I'd dropped from my lack of interest in food, I felt comfortable in my bikini again, as long as I remained conservatively wrapped in my kimono when heading to the pool on the roof-top of my building. Gautam was busy with work during the day, and I needed a distraction while the puppy took her late-morning nap.

I staked out an ideal spot far from the shallow toddler pool. Above me, the sun looked promising, and I was instantly reassured that getting out of my dark apartment would be good for me.

I placed the large cooler on the ground next to my lounge chair. No one needed to know the cooler was full of beer, a water bottle, and a meticulously sliced and salted cucumber. After reclining on the lounger, I dug into the cooler and filled my insulated cup with a beer.

I put on my headphones to mute the shrills

of toddlers, a sound that caused my mind to slip into a chaotic spin of longing. Then, as the sun rose and burst from the clouds, I pulled out the psychological thriller I was reading. The heroine needed to find a way out of captivity to survive. As I rolled onto my stomach, I hoped no one would see how the bikini bottom rode up my ass.

After hours in the sun, a heavy buzz numbed my pain, and I pulled my cover-up back on. I didn't know when I'd feel happy again, but I felt content with the sunlight, distraction, and buzz, and as the tiles baked in the sun, a trail of sweat ran down my spine. For a moment, I felt like I'd found a way out of the fog, like I could make it through the summer.

It was about time to take Ella for a walk, so I gathered my belongings and entered the elevator with a few other residents.

"Sorry to interrupt, but how is your baby?" a lady asked as the doors closed in on us, blocking all chance of escape. She was a nutritionist in her early thirties and exclusively wore workout apparel. She often snuck her little dog into the pool, despite the building's ban on poolside pets.

"What was that?" I figured I must have misheard her. Her dog flopped onto the cool tile of the elevator.

"Is your baby allowed outside yet?"

I cringed in horror. Allowed outside yet? Did she assume I'd locked my baby away in my apartment over the past few months? The thought was so obscene that I bit the inside of my cheek to hold back my laughter. If only I could have been an outsider looking into our tragedy and not living in it.

"I'm sorry. We lost her." I didn't know why I apologized nor why I couldn't find the right words to explain that our baby had died. I *lost* my baby sounded gentler, as if there were still a possibility my baby could be found one day.

"Oh," she said. "I'm so sorry."

The other neighbors squirmed, and no one said a word until the elevator doors opened again, offering release.

Weeks later, when I went to my first support group meeting, I shared my propensity for these clipped elevator conversations, only to make the group of grieving parents erupt with laughter. If you haven't heard this kind of noise before, strangers with holes in their hearts laughing together, it's the most beautiful sound in the world.

CHAPTER SIXTEEN

When the undertaker called, it was the thick of summer. The asphalt blazed under the unforgiving sun. I quickly hooked Ella's leash and collar and hurried out to meet him on the street corner. I slid off my flip-flops for a moment to test the heat of the concrete to ensure Ella wouldn't burn her paws. Too hot. We navigated to the other side of the street, which had shade from the buildings.

One of the roads was closed for construction, so I had to walk two blocks to meet the undertaker in front of Starbucks. He got out of the Lincoln Town Car and kept his hazards on, implying it'd be a quick transaction. I was almost offended that he didn't want to park and stay longer to console me as I received her.

He looked too young, maybe in his mid-twenties, to be an undertaker. Then again, maybe I looked too young to be a bereaved mother at the age of twenty-five. He placed the small white cardboard box, sealed in a plastic freezer bag, in my hands. It weighed less than the cremated remains of my family's fifteen-year-old cat. Even the urn for my cat had been nicer, wooden with a gold plate engraved with the cat's name: Magic.

I had expected that, for three hundred dollars, I'd at least get a suitable urn.

Despite the pathetic appearance of this box, I had never needed something so badly. I wanted to fall to my knees when he gave me my daughter. Instead, I took the box and thanked him as if this wasn't the strangest transaction of my life. With Ella by my side, her long pink tongue dangling, we walked back home. I clutched my daughter's ashes to my heart.

When I returned, Gautam helped me find a place to store her ashes.

"Be careful," he said as I removed the plastic bag to get to her box. "Here, let me." He gently pulled my hand away.

As he carefully handled the ashes, I was reminded that his father had been cremated. In his culture, cremation was the standard except for the death of a baby. Babies were buried, I later learned.

We opened up the memorial box together, placed her box of ashes inside, and returned it to my closet. One day, we would get a better urn. One day, we would spread her ashes.

Even years later, we never did. I remain afraid that if the sealed box is opened, particles of her ashes will fly into the air, and I'll be left with less of her, that the funeral parlor will accidentally drop her box when transferring her to the urn. We considered spreading her ashes on the second anniversary of her death, when we went for a vacation to Jackson Hole, Wyoming, but I worried that it was too far away. What if I missed her and wanted to visit the spot where we'd left her?

To this day, she remains in the same spot, in my closet near my handbags.

In therapy, I learned how to cope with what people said to me. There are strategies, like giving a compliment first before you say how you really feel. I had to see the good in their consoling efforts and even qualities I admired. My therapist wouldn't let me write people off because they said things we agreed were horrible, like, "I guess we will never know what could have happened if you'd gone to the hospital sooner," something I was told days after our daughter's death.

My therapist shared that outsiders fantasize that babies can be saved. We like to believe that we have control over our fate. There was no way to save our baby. As a nurse told me in a support group, when babies die, it's a matter of seconds. There's no way to spontaneously bring a baby who died in utero back to life.

Others said, "You can always have another baby," and, "you're so young." I think I even told myself that at first. I might have even started that horrible mantra, which spread throughout my family's and friends' advice on the matter. But the fact is, there is nothing to say to make anyone feel better after they've lost a child.

Many things were wrong with that logic. First, there was no guarantee or assurance that we would have another living, healthy baby. We could have a miscarriage, another stillbirth, or infant death. It could be even worse the next time. We didn't know. Because the doctors couldn't find anything, it meant that some things were ruled out, while other things we would never know.

Or sure, we might get lucky and "have another" baby, but it would never be Laila. And if we did have this future baby, I'd always be reminded of the older sister they would never get to meet. The new baby would never be the same beautiful girl I had seen. They wouldn't have her fluttering heartbeats and kicks that kept me strong and alive for our seven months together. Other pregnancies would never be my first, new territory, scary, stressful, and invigorating. I'd never feel as lucky as I had before; now, in the back of my mind, I'd be ill-fated and not a youthful, healthy girl bound to have a living, breathing, healthy baby.

And when I thought, *No one understands me*, it was true. No one could understand what Gautam and I had shared with Laila, those joyful moments and the moments when I'd cried and cooed to her that I would do anything for her. No one could understand how we had been robbed of that.

One of my closest friends visited me. I had known her since the fifth grade. On the same day Laila had died, I had called this friend only to find out that her family dog had also died. It had been a bad day for us, and best not to bring it up again. When I offered her a drink, her green eyes flickered curiously.

"It's 10 a.m," she said in a soft voice.

"Oh, right. You don't mind if I do?" I asked as I grabbed a beer from my fridge.

"No, go ahead," she replied with a look of concern. I was used to it. Everyone was concerned about me.

We went to the pool together, and I kept drinking. I wore the same kimono and packed my bag full of beer. I didn't bring food, but the heavy cooler pulled sharply on my right shoulder. My friend noticed me struggling with the bag, and she held it for me. We navigated to a spot away from other people, although not many had trickled in yet.

My friend left a few hours later, and due to my empty stomach, I was already feeling the buzz as I drank my beer from my coffee mug. The sun broke out of the clouds and lingered on my body. For company, I read a memoir about a young girl held captive by her own parents to be an intellectual prodigy. People made me sick; not everyone deserved to be parents. When I got to the part of the story where the girl escapes, I spotted a neighbor walking over who knew about our loss; he was shirtless and wore paisley swim trunks.

He sat down on the chaise lounge next to me. "How are you?" he asked as he eyed my cooler.

What a loaded question, I thought. *Barely hanging in there. Somehow alive.*

"OK," I said as I returned to my book.

"Do you have the summer off?" he asked.

"I do." I wanted to read and not have a conversation.

"It must be nice to have the summer off. When I had the summer off in between jobs, I'd come up here and drink."

My face went hot when I realized he had noticed there was beer in my coffee mug. There was nothing nice about being off from work for the reason I was, but he didn't need to know this. I returned to my book.

The death of a child can ruin marriages, but we got married again. We had planned to have the traditional Indian reception after Laila arrived. We would have celebrated with all of our relatives around Laila, our beautiful little girl. We still planned the event, hoping that being around family and celebrating our love would lift our spirits. My mother-in-law generously treated us to the event. She rented out an Indian restaurant, hired a DJ, and got a beautiful florist to decorate the tables. I selected the color of the plates and bows around the chairs, a light purple, my favorite.

The day before the wedding, I became trapped in my bridal lehenga when I tried it on. The tight, sequined teal fabric felt like a corset around my chest.

"Gautam!" I yelped like an injured dog. "I'm stuck."

He smirked. "Get changed. My mom will

take you to the seamstress."

I threw on the only pair of jeans that fit and left with my mother-in-law. In my panic, I failed to grab a jacket to cover my belly shirt. I looked ridiculous, like a nineties pop star. When the dressmaker led me to the small dressing room and released me from the top, I felt as if I could breathe again. She was able to conduct an emergency zipper repair.

That evening, Gautam hired a henna artist to do my bridal mehendi. As I waited for it to dry in the living room at Komal's house, a pregnant cousin started to talk about her future baby, and my throat tightened. Every story about a baby caused me to tremble. I thought about what had been stolen from us, and I ran from the living room and cried in the guest bedroom with wet henna on my arms. Gautam rubbed my back, careful to make sure the wet designs on my arms didn't get ruined.

"Do you think you can head back downstairs to get your arms finished?" he asked.

"I can do that," I said, although I didn't want to.

I returned to an empty living room. The artist came in. "Did you not like the mehindi?" she asked, looking hurt.

"It's beautiful," I said as I looked down at my arms, covered in the intricate designs. "I just lost my baby."

"Oh, dear," she said and continued working on my arms. "I'm so sorry," she hummed.

My mother-in-law was worried; maybe the

event was too soon. I assured her that I was fine. The wedding was the perfect excuse to get dressed up and even pretend for one night that our world wasn't crumbling down.

At the wedding, relatives gifted me with gold necklaces. I looked for Laila everywhere, in the arms of recent mothers with their babies. She was missing.

I wrote a speech about Laila, which I shared with everyone:

It's a pleasure meeting and seeing the faces of the community that raised this wonderful man I have married. I'd like to thank my mother-in-law, Malini, for putting this beautiful event together, as well as my sister-in-law, Komal, who somehow managed to find time she didn't have to make this celebration perfect.

And of course, I thank my husband, who has been devoted and by my side during the hardest time in my life.

Today is a bittersweet day.

As many of you know, and for those of you who do not know, exactly three months ago, on March 9, 2018, at 1:28 p.m., I gave birth to a beautiful girl weighing one pound and 7.1 ounces and thirteen inches long.

You wouldn't have thought anything was wrong when we held her. The only thing that made her different was that she did not scream or cry when she was born; she simply was peacefully asleep. She looked like her father.

The doctors are still unsure why the baby passed away during a perfectly healthy pregnancy. When we found out that day that she didn't have a heartbeat, the doctors had to induce labor.

Although it was a painful, complicated, and traumatic experience, my husband and my parents were there for me those two days. When my husband and I left the hospital without a baby in my arms, I didn't think I'd ever be able to heal from the loss of our daughter.

In three days, Monday, June 11, would be Laila's due date.

It's been a very trying three months, but my husband has been there each step of the way. I wake up blessed because we are parents to a perfect child, who loved us unconditionally as much as we love and care for her.

She brought us together in a way that I'm forever grateful, because I know that no matter what we go through, it will never compare to what we lost, and we are bound forever because somehow, through the darkness, we are navigating this loss together.

The morning after I delivered Laila, right before Gautam and I left the hospital, a popular song started to play in the back of my mind. Ed Sheeran's song, "Photograph."

I grabbed my phone to play the song. Gautam and I listened to the song as we held each other and looked at Philadelphia's skyline through the hospital window.

If you listen closely to these lyrics that I am about to share with you, I believe our daughter is trying to communicate with us; she wants us to know she lives forever in our hearts.

Thank you.

As we danced to Ed Sheeran's song "Photograph," Gautam stiffened up, frozen from the heavy emotion the speech had brought forth. I pulled him close, leaning on him. Laila was celebrated that night.

Her due date passed, and I was so sad without her there. She was gone, but she lived everywhere.

Happiness is fleeting. Shortly after the wedding reception, we received the full autopsy report in the mail. My therapist said it "reopened my grief." Once you think you've gotten better, things can rip your heart open again.

According to the autopsy, our Laila, at twenty-six weeks and four days of gestation, possibly had a sudden and acute episode of asphyxiation from a potential blood clot in the umbilical cord. They believe she may have died twenty-four to forty-eight hours before I made it to the doctor. They could tell when she died by the color of her skin. The report discussed in detail how perfect she had been.

That means, when I called the nurse about my baby, Laila was already dead. A hospital trip wouldn't have accomplished anything. Now when I think about that moment, when I was clipping Ernie the plant, I like to imagine that I was there and present with her, hands to belly, when her brave little soul left this world.

I read the report on the kitchen table with Gautam close, hunched over the papers. On one of the final pages, I read that she had black hair, only a centimeter long. I lost myself, sobbing for at least thirty minutes straight until my eyes became puffy and swollen. I never knew she had hair; I didn't take off her knit hat that she wore at the hospital. I didn't think she would have black hair like Gautam, and the idea of how beautiful she would have grown up to be destroyed me.

Years later, I'd find a single strand of her black hair trapped beneath the pink knit hat she'd worn, which caused me to erupt in the same uncontrollable tears.

CHAPTER SEVENTEEN

I wasn't the first griever who'd decided to run as a way to heal. One runner shared on her blog her experience running her first marathon. She described how, when she neared the finish line, it felt like she was with her sibling who had passed away. She hallucinated him and saw him smiling at her. She could feel his warmth; it felt like he was hugging her.

Despite all of those gifts of second sight I had inherited, I never saw Laila in my waking life. This frustrated me. I'd spent all of those years scared of my closet because of the ghosts I'd seen hiding in there at night, but I couldn't even see my own daughter. But if I ran a *marathon*, surely, I would. I was convinced that God, or whoever it was up above, would suddenly like me or favor me when I completed the course. That on race day, the sky would open and my daughter would appear at the finish line. I'd have one more chance to hold her again. I'd hoped that the climax of running the marathon would lead me back to her, even if only for one ethereal minute, so I could hold her in my arms again.

In mid-June, I signed up for the Philadelphia Marathon and began a twenty-week marathon training program.

I went to the pool again, and when I returned to the apartment, my head was spinning from all the beers I'd had. Gautam noticed the clink of the beer cans that I dumped from the cooler into the recycling. In the bathroom, I splashed cool water on my face. I had forgotten sunscreen, and I was burnt.

"Don't you have a group run?" he asked as he noted the time on the kitchen stove.

"Oh, shit," I said, and I grabbed an empty glass left out on the bathroom sink, filled it with water, and chugged the water down. "Thanks for reminding me."

I swirled around mouthwash so the runners wouldn't notice my breath, which reeked of booze.

I couldn't believe I had forgotten about the group run. I had tried my best to attend these runs each Thursday night at the local shoe store. Sometimes the runs were packed with twenty to thirty runners. The energy of the group inspired me more than I would have been on my own.

I could smell the alcohol coming out of my pores as I ran in the ninety-degree weather. I felt sick and fell towards the back of the pack. A woman nearby was training for her first 10k race at the end of the summer. She wore a thick black backpack full of water. I was desperate for a sip.

I breathed in the dry air, and my lungs felt tight. I could barely make out all the runners. Lesson learned: there was no way I could day drink again with my daily runs.

I need to get my shit together if I really want to do this race.

On my next run, I was sober and hydrated. The weather was boiling, over ninety degrees in the morning sun. I ran in shorts and a tank-top along Boathouse Row, where historic townhomes for college crew teams line the water. There was a weekend regatta, and I had to run on and off the pavement to avoid crew teams carrying their boats. My mouth watered at the lemonade and hot dog stands.

My thighs didn't burn together as much now that I knew to apply copious amounts of Vaseline and powder. My stride felt light, and my body was happy with me. It was a short run today. I felt determined. I felt different. The sun spilled lazily over the river, and the reflection warmed my shoulders like a big, gentle hug.

I was scared to run in the mornings. Horror tales of gropey men who followed women along the river trail were frequently told by the women runners I had met in the group run. There were stories like the Schuylkill River stabber, who, a few years ago, had attacked a runner along the trail. All occurrences seemed to happen early in the morning, when the trail was empty.

While I didn't have much of a desire to live, I was terrified at the idea of another horrible thing happening to me. I often waited during the day to run until 5 p.m., the most popular after-work time, when the trail was full.

My brother runs when the night is so dark it swallows you. He was back from college for the summer, and I went to my parents' house to spend the night. I had my first twelve-mile run on my training plan, and I needed someone to run with.

We used our phones as flashlights, as the overgrown brambles caught our ankles. We crossed a quiet highway intersection with a slow pedestrian light and ran through a park where we'd both used to race in high school.

He was now a college cross-country runner, but he ran slowly alongside me to motivate me, although it looked like it was painful for him to shorten his long stride and crawl along at my pace. We finished the run together.

Sometimes after runs, I felt bruised. My eyes burned with fatigue, and my legs boiled with lactic acid. I struggled to take Ella out for walks after my runs, so Gautam took most of the responsibility from me. I tweaked my left knee, making the surrounding muscles feel unsteady.

It was now early August, four more months until the marathon. I kept chugging along at a slow, painful, thirteen- or fourteen-minute pace for each mile. My stride was a gentle crawl. Sometimes a short run could take over an hour. I kept taking deep breaths, knowing nothing could hurt more than losing her.

⁕⁕⁕

Down the street from Komal's house, I discovered the Washington and Old Dominion Trail.

Running the trail now reminded me of back when I'd been planning to have a baby, when Gautam and I had felt a range of emotions, like excitement and fear, all at once. Now there was nothing but emptiness.

Unlike the trail in Philly, I felt safe enough to run this one at dawn. The trail was beautiful, its thick black pavement stretching through Falls Church, Vienna, and into the city of Arlington. I did my first sixteen-mile run there for my marathon training program. Vendors had set up stands in a local market, and children participated in a fall festival. I went to use the cement bathroom open to the public, which felt like a luxury compared to porta-potties. There wasn't a mirror to look at myself while I washed my hands, but the water was warm, and I splashed some on my face.

I listened to an audiobook as I ran, and I was consistently hitting eleven-minute-mile splits. It was my longest training run so far, and I felt strong, but I was out of water. I called Gautam, and he said he'd bike along the trail until he found me.

My mouth was dry, and the summer sun shone

down. I kept my eyes peeled on the pathway for bikers in the distance. Every time I spotted one, I hoped it was Gautam.

Then, in the distance, I saw him. He was on his nephew's bike, and the sight caused me to buckle over mid-run with laughter. The bike was so small that it caused his knees to spread out to the sides, and his basketball shorts were hiked up his thighs.

"How are you even biking like that? Doesn't it hurt?" I said as I took sips of the lemon-lime Gatorade.

"I couldn't find Komal's bike and was in a rush. I didn't want you to dehydrate out here."

He biked alongside me as I jogged the last few miles.

***

We were invited to a birthday party for Laila's cousin. If Laila had lived, the kids would have been one year apart from each other. I didn't want to go.

"I don't know if I can handle seeing kids," I told Gautam.

I could immediately see the disappointment on his face. Family was so important to him.

"Do you think you can try for me?" he asked.

I didn't want to disappoint him anymore. I would try for him, and he promised we could leave early if I needed to.

And we brought Ella with us. When we arrived, she joyfully explored the home, wiggling her nub tail.

When I walked into the living room, I froze. There was a handful of toddlers there. I felt the way I did every time I saw the newborn who lived in our condo building. I'd tremble at the sight, even when the baby was tucked away in a stroller, and turn my head from it.

Things seemed to slow down at the sound of baby laughter, giggles, cries, screams. My mind glazed over at the sight of toys, plastic teacups, plastic pizza, stuffed giraffes and llamas, all things Laila would have played with and shoved into her mouth with the others. Cinderella sniffed all the objects, sneaking in licks of the toddler's hands.

I wanted to run out of that room, but it wasn't the babies' fault or their parents'. It wasn't my fault. I had to be strong. Ella sat by my side during the party, and we left early.

I told my therapist. My therapist's sister-in-law had birthed a stillborn son at full-term, and now she couldn't be around babies, including my therapist's. I didn't want to suffer from the same problem, but I didn't know how I could cope. Years later, she adopted a child and became comfortable around other kids.

There was no set rule or time for when I would feel comfortable again, my therapist advised me.

$$\sim\!\!\sim\!\!\sim\!\!\sim\!\!\sim$$

I would have to work soon. The summer was ending, and I'd been off for close to three months. Ironically, I'd been away from work longer than I would have if I'd taken my maternity leave.

I was nervous about going back, but I told

myself it would be better this time. I had my running shoes and my GPS watch to focus on at the end of each day, and I'd be rewarded by the fresh air, the heel-toe thumping on pavement, and my makeup running off my face from sweat.

I dreamed I had another stillborn. I was in a hospital room, and when the nurse asked if I wanted to hold the baby, I said, "Yes, yes, please bring her to me."

When I held her, she wasn't Laila. She was at least eight to nine pounds, with a round, pudgy face wrapped in a thin pink blanket. It hit me then that this was Laila's younger sister, whom I had been thinking of having when Gautam and I discussed trying again.

In my dream, I held this baby tightly, lovingly, longingly, making sure she knew she was safe. Was it my subconscious preparing me for something the future might bring, a future baby sister?

The weather was ninety degrees on the river trail, and my body caved into a slow, stumbling pace. I ran four miles and felt depleted. The sports drink didn't help. My time was off, too slow. I feared I wouldn't make the time cut-off for the race. My music didn't pump me up; I was winded.

A freight train thundered past the trail, and a hot wind flooded my lungs. I felt vacant. Running a marathon felt impossible.

I took a break from running over the weekend and let my depleted muscles rest. The past two Sundays, I had done thirteen-plus-mile runs. This weekend, I slept; I was supposed to do an eight-mile run, but I didn't. Instead, I took an hour-long yoga class.

In the evening, I treated Gautam to dinner on Broad Street, and then I went to bed early.

I also watched movies. I took long naps. Gautam cleaned the apartment. We did four loads of laundry, and I folded our items, but didn't put them away. Gautam scrubbed the bathroom until it gleamed from the bleach. I took a long, hot shower and shaved. We went grocery shopping.

It was the dog and us. It was only us.

One Saturday, I scheduled an eight-mile loop around Kelly Drive. When I got to the trailhead, my legs felt heavy from the shock of training, and I ended up walking. I peered across the Schuylkill River, and the bright clouds reflected off the murky water. I felt at peace, far away from grief, as I walked those miles in the sun. I was so slow that Martin Luther King Drive opened up to traffic, as it does at noon, and I walked as fast as I could so I wouldn't get hit by a car.

When I finally got back to our apartment, salt covered my face, and I was drenched in sweat. The early morning had shifted into a hot summer afternoon.

"How did it take you three hours?" Gautam asked as he stood by the door. "I almost had to go looking for you."

"I'm slow. Don't worry," I said and then guzzled down the nearest glass of water.

He still did.

My extended leave ended, and I was a zombie back at work. It was odd, because I knew I wasn't as bad as I had been months ago, but working at a place where everyone knew my story was difficult. I was assigned easy projects to help with my transition back, but this almost made it worse since I didn't have anything to keep my mind busy. My coworkers were kind and happy I was back, but I still felt like the office crazy lady, the woman in the attic in *Jane Eyre*.

In my inbox, I received a new job opportunity from a recruiter, and I scheduled the interview for the next week. A new job. I ran the idea by Gautam, and he was encouraging. It was with a good company. In fact, he had interviewed at the company when he'd been looking to work somewhere more stable than a start-up before we welcomed Laila into the world. I hadn't even realized he'd done that for us.

It felt good to be excited again about something. For the first time, I felt motivated and like I was moving my career forward. Maybe the rocky hurdles I'd been managing at my current job wouldn't exist at a larger company.

I was surprised by how motivated I was to try

and get this new job. I felt like a different person. I'd had jobs I'd wanted to leave before, but I'd become very complacent. In this case, I was very optimistic and found myself enthusiastically moving forward.

Gautam helped prepare me for the interview process, since he was familiar with the private-equity industry. When I was in the bath, he would sit on the toilet and ask me questions.

"What makes you a good candidate?"

"What are your strengths and weaknesses?"

"Why is this role good for you?"

Each night, I got better at the responses. When it came time for the real interview, a three-hour-long process, I left feeling optimistic. Change was coming.

Don't cry before bed. If you do, have a skin-care routine that helps reduce puffiness, like eye cream and icing your eyes, or else, for work the following morning, you'll look like you have severe allergies.

I cried because I didn't run after work. Running helps, but it was a rest day. I hadn't taken one in a while, and my body needed it. It's important to rest while marathon training. But my mind kept running, and my sadness drained my body. I showered and clung to Laila's keepsake box.

I couldn't have the keepsake box out when Gautam was around. It upset him to see it. When he went to meet his friend, I grabbed it. I looked through anatomy ultrasound pictures, gazing at her perfect feet and head. In one picture, her hands were reaching out to the screen, like she was waving at me. My thumb looked gigantic as it rested on the image of her hand.

On my twenty-sixth birthday, I had my first twenty-mile run. It was strange to think that only a year ago, I had been saying yes under the northern lights and I'd thought I'd have my daughter with me when I turned twenty-six.

This was the longest run of my entire marathon training program before the race. I was so worried about it, and I didn't think I could do it. Would it rain? What if the group I was running with didn't have somebody who ran at my pace? What if my stomach hurt? What if there weren't any restrooms?

When I arrived outside of the art museum, I met a woman with jet-black hair who looked as nervous as I did. She was running with headphones on, so I listened to the sound of our feet striking the ground. On the third mile, halfway down Martin Luther King Drive, she waited for me when I had to use the restroom. There was only one lonesome port-a-potty, which smelled terrible. I had to squat on wobbly legs, but it was better than nothing.

I also didn't rinse my water bottle properly, and the soapy taste ruined my water, so we stopped at each water stop. We parted ways at mile nineteen, and then I ran the last mile home alone. I felt like I could have kept running. I picked up my pace and smiled. It never did rain, and the weather held out as a picture-perfect overcast for running.

I dreamed I was holding a big, brown-eyed baby girl. She felt so warm on my chest and was wearing a light pink floral cotton onesie. I changed her diaper; I was in a big house. As I went from room to room, I realized it was the house of a childhood friend, which had a large loft upstairs. I was humming as I held the baby. This baby wasn't Laila, but I knew she was mine.

Would this future baby visit us again and be awake, happy, and healthy? Was it a sign to try again? A sign that Laila's little sister was coming soon and she'd be well? My mother told me she'd had the same dream of a beautiful and happy baby and that she knew this wasn't Laila, but the baby was mine.

"I hope not soon. I don't feel ready," I said.

"I know the timing will be perfect for you," she replied.

Baby, if this is you, let me know when you want to come home. Before you go, tell Laila I love her and I'm still her mommy, although we are on different sides.

I landed the new job. To celebrate, Gautam took me out for drinks.

"To a fresh start," he said.

A fresh start. I was eager to be at a big

company where no one knew my story. I was no longer going to be in a small office of only ten people, all of whom knew the excruciating details of what had happened. I'd left my old job on good terms, and everyone had hugged me goodbye.

My new job required a commute, not a walk to the office. I had to take the city bus to the outskirts of the city. I was working hard, studying the new industry I was in. I woke up early, sometimes at dawn, and got home late, when it was dark and cold. I felt like I was pushing myself and that I needed it. I was also meeting new people. Unlike at my last job, they were close in age with me, and we cracked jokes at our desks. A part of me felt young again. Another part of me thought, *If you only knew what happened to me five months ago.*

On Friday evenings, the bus never showed up on time. I waited as traffic passed underneath the bus shelter. The commute made me feel a little more human again, like I was working towards something, although I didn't know what it was.

On one of my runs after work, I ran by a couple with two toddlers who had full cheeks and freckles. The dad, wearing a green cotton shirt with gaping sweat stains, was arguing with his wife. Most likely, the family was leaving or going to the Franklin Institute—a museum for kids. One of its famous attractions was the larger-than-life heart, where you could walk through the heart's chambers. My mother had experienced a bout of claustrophobia when she'd taken me there as a little girl.

"It was Eve's fault, girls. She ate the forbidden fruit," he said as he stopped the girls to wait at the crosswalk for the light to turn green.

"I disagree. You shouldn't tell the girls this," the mother replied in an irritated tone as she wiped the sweat from the back of her neck.

"Why shouldn't I? It's the truth. It's Eve's fault. She took a bite from the apple when she wasn't supposed to."

When the crosswalk light turned green, the wife huffed and grabbed the girls' hands. One girl tried to escape her grip. The couple made parenting look miserable. I smiled because I wasn't a part of it and was running. I was grateful for the loud parents because they didn't make me feel envious or like I was missing anything.

"Hold Mommy's hand!" the mother shrieked before they crossed the street.

But the topic was a good one. *Original sin.* My mother had become obsessed with original sin after Laila's death. She worried that since only a minister, not a priest, had baptized Laila, my baby had original sin. The priest wasn't available to come to our room, which my mother was furious about. I wanted to ask her about this obsession, if she *really* thought Laila was in hell. She spoke to the priest at her church after Laila died, and he assured her that children who died before they were born had no original sin, that her soul was saved and she didn't even need to be baptized to go to heaven. My mother was relieved, and I was annoyed that she seriously thought like that.

However, I had my own obsession with sin. My mind raced with the blame a lot, not with respect to Eve or original sin, but with mothers in general. So many moms who lost a child blame themselves. One mother I met believed her baby had died because she'd carried something heavy right before the miscarriage. I, too, had reasons why I was responsible for Laila's death: I'd eaten sushi a few times, though my OB-GYN approved of the raw fish as long as it was high quality; I'd gotten blonde highlights for the wedding in the second trimester; I'd had a sip of champagne after we got married and swirled it around my mouth, trying to remember what it tasted like or why I'd once liked drinking so much; I'd gone on a kayaking tour with my husband in Arizona; I hadn't worked out at all while pregnant because I'd been worried it would hurt the baby; I'd ridden in planes. I didn't go to the hospital sooner.

Years later, my second pregnancy looked a lot different. I had no sushi, no sips of champagne, and I didn't dye my hair. I didn't travel, either. In fact, I scarcely left my house at all since we were in the middle of a global pandemic. I got in my thirty minutes of exercise nearly every day. I swam laps in my building's pool. I even had to stop drinking alcohol and took prenatal vitamins for months leading up to my conception since I was on Clomid to help with fertility.

I still acted like I was to blame—that, like Eve, it had been my fault all along. It started to rain, and I could hear the squeals of the kids, though I was down the block now.

The rain was thick and wet, and most people didn't seem to mind. In Philly, most of the crowds accepted their bad luck. Only a few people ran to take cover. I couldn't catch up to a woman with Whole Foods bags and flip-flops before she ran into her house. I thought I had a good pace going, too. I hoped I wasn't too slow for the upcoming marathon, if I couldn't finish the race under a certain time, the course officials would take me off the course.

Sometimes I'd ask Gautam what he thought to see how he would react to the idea of having more kids. It was my version of a test to see how compatible we were and if we could endure what had happened to us.

"What if I never wanted to have a baby again?" I asked him, pushing him on purpose, expecting him to not want to be with me if I didn't want to have any more kids.

"Then we will figure it out."

"What if I want to wait a few years?"

"How many?"

"Three?"

"I think two is better."

"What if it happens again?"

"It won't."

He always said the right things and passed this test I gave him.

I hopped around various support groups, trying

to find the perfect fit. Families came and went, which made it hard to get a sense of community. On good days, I connected with a family. In an off session, it sometimes felt like a twisted competition of who had lost their baby later or in a more complicated way. Sometimes Gautam would be by my side. Other days, he wanted to stay home with the dog.

The first time, it was hard to tell Laila's story to strangers. With enough practice, I got better and less choked up when I talked about her life. In these groups, I learned that some men and women can grieve differently. I heard from the women with partners who didn't understand them, boyfriends who didn't want to hold the baby or husbands who seemed to be able to move on with their life. Then there was the other kind, that taught me how men and women can grieve the same, or even harder. One woman who had suffered a loss attended the meeting with her husband. Her husband loved talking about holding his little girl and how much his daughter resembled his wife.

My favorite group was at the hospital I'd given birth in. At first, I struggled to go there because I was worried I'd feel too traumatized to set foot in the building again. While it was surreal walking into the building, this ended up being my best group.

I told the group that I had signed up for a marathon to honor my daughter, and the group liked that. One person had competed in a triathlon for his daughter. His wife shared how she had signed up for a bereavement retreat in a group session called Return to Zero: H.O.P.E. The founder had made a movie called *Return to Zero*, and she now held healing retreats. This year, it was in Colorado. I made a mental note to look into it.

CHAPTER EIGHTEEN

A week before my marathon, foot pain set in. On the first weekend in November, I ran a 10k race in Camden, New Jersey. Half of the race took place on the Ben Franklin Bridge. There was a steep decline while coming down the bridge, and a sharp pain radiated under my heel at mile three. I could have stopped and played it safe, but I was running my 5k pace. I felt fast. I felt all of my hard training was paying off.

The following day, my foot was swollen and hard to walk on from the pain, so I squeezed in light cardio during my lunch hour to give it a break. Despite my best efforts at keeping weight off my arch, the pain persisted. I needed to see a professional, especially since I was scheduled to run my first marathon on Sunday.

I was the only one in my new office's small gym that day, pumping my legs on the stationary bike as sweat formed on my neck. I tried my best to visualize running on the trails that gave me freedom, but instead, I was left with two options: staring at my reflection in the wall-length mirror or keeping track of time on my watch. I kept my head down, counting down the minutes until the end.

Eventually, my watch buzzed, celebrating the fact that I'd hit the twenty minutes I needed. With a good bit of tension released, I walked across the black rubber tiles to grab the paper towel and cleaning spray. Then I wiped the circular sweat marks off the bike's seat and tossed the towel into the bin.

Across the hall in the locker room, I stood beside the shower curtain, trying to choose between my only water options: boiling or freezing. Since I was already shaking from nerves, cold it was. I re-adjusted the curtain to hide myself, fearful as always that a coworker might catch sight of my body through the crack. I was self-conscious of my postpartum body.

I made quick work of showering and drying off and then slid into my bright pink bodycon dress and blazer, which made me look like a newscaster. The finance industry had an unspoken preppy dress code; business casual often meant designer clothes for women. To play it safe at my new job, I wanted to look good, so I dressed in cheerful colors that gave me a headache.

I needed to leave right after lunch to get to my podiatrist on time. Since losing Laila, doctor visits set me on edge. Even scheduling a visit with the podiatrist left me with feelings of inadequacy— it was all my fault that my body was failing me. Again.

Back at my cubicle, I packed up my belongings. I couldn't help but smile at the photo I had taped to my desk wall of Gautam's and my first dance for our Indian wedding. When I had bad days, the picture proved how much we still loved each other after all our pain.

"Leaving early?" a co-worker asked from across the open office space. He was a younger guy who ran a tight ship and had appointed himself captain. I didn't mind; I was even flattered to be treated like the others.

"Doctor's appointment," I said as I unplugged my laptop and dropped it into my shoulder bag. I was happy for the fresh start. No one knew my story yet, and it was liberating to be viewed as a regular twenty-six-year-old. Deep down, grief had aged me to my mid-fifties; having your daughter's ashes in your closet tends to have that outcome.

"Let me know if you need help while you're out," he said and returned his gaze to his dual monitors. I beamed, although it made my jaw ache. I had never worked at a large company with a team before, and the support made a difference.

Out of the office, I squinted in the sunlight to let my eyes adjust. It was the time of year when the sun set early, drawing me into total darkness by the time I usually finished work each day. The nice, sunny fall weather depressed me. I preferred downpours and storms, when everyone looked as miserable as I felt. I crossed the overpass with a view of City Live Avenue, a strip of fast-food chain restaurants, a few other office spaces like mine, and, off in the distance, a grocery store. My new office location was less than ideal compared to the crimson high-rise I'd once worked in, but

I didn't mind commuting to the Philly suburbs. Spotting the faint lights from the bus in the distance, I quickened my pace while trying to keep the weight off my arch.

Within minutes, I had stuffed myself into the back of the city bus. As the bus zipped down the highway, I tottered my way to a window seat. The alternative was the dreaded aisle seat, where the only place to gaze off and stare was into the eyes of another passenger.

Through the window, drivers on one of the most dangerous highways in the city gave me something to see. One in a sedan bobbed her head to music as she strummed her fingers on the wheel, sporadically cursing at the top of her lungs. Another in a Toyota talked on the phone and slammed his brakes as the driver in front of him switched lanes. I longed to be like those drivers, to have a normal life again, to get angry about the little things, like traffic, and not feel completely consumed by grieving the death of my baby.

I plugged in my headphones to mute the grinding gears, heavy breathers, and loud talkers, but nothing quieted the thoughts racing through my mind. If I couldn't run the marathon on Sunday, I didn't know what I'd do. Having that race in my sights had given me hope all of those months. Without it, I worried that sorrow would consume me like a vulture, leaving nothing but bones.

As we approached my stop, I yanked the lever that chimed the bell. Then I squeezed through other passengers and limped down Chestnut Street. The colors of fall shadowed me as I reached the office and buzzed myself in. On the elevator, I held my breath, sweating bullets, bracing for the worst. From my experience, medical practices were the bearers of bad news.

The receptionist's acrylic nails clacked against the desktop keyboard, putting me on edge. Her soft pop music played from a static-laced radio as she passed me the cardboard intake forms. I filled out my information and circled number seven on the Stanford pain scale. If the scale had been for emotional pain, I'd well have exceeded the maximum of ten. I returned it to her desk and handed over my insurance card. Experience had led me to enroll in the premium plan, even though it crushed my paycheck. I no longer trusted my body—who knew when it would land me in the hospital again—and I didn't need more medical bills like last time. That was the one thing I knew for sure. I could do nothing about the past, I thought as I glanced at her desk, filled with baby pictures, but at least I was now well insured against future disaster.

She caught me looking and turned down her radio. "My grandbabies," she said, smiling.

I pursed my lips. I still struggled with kid-focused conversations. When the situation arose, I pictured myself looking ghostly pale, disheveled, scarred, and awkward, like Tim Burton's *Edward Scissorhands*.

Taking the cue, she returned my card, smacking green gum against her chapped lips. "Okay, I have everything I need. You can head to the back office."

I claimed a chair in the examination room and crinkled the paper beneath my hands. Across from me, a framed poster displayed a colorful anatomical chart identifying the many parts of a foot. Without warning, images of my daughter's little feet flashed in my mind, and just like that, my heart traced the small ink prints the hospital had given me. I wanted her footprints tattooed on my shoulder next. Staring at that chart, a pang of regret hit me. At her birth, I'd been too afraid to touch her hands and feet. She'd seemed so fragile. So frail. The staff had swaddled her in the fluffy pink blanket instead, and I'd held her in my arms, trying to shield her, to keep her warm. Safe.

The paper crinkled beneath me as I squirmed and fought to hold back tears. I was tempted to bolt back onto the street and find my way home, but the podiatrist entered, bringing a warm smile with her. She gently tugged off my sock, and I flinched at the touch of her cold hands. "Tell me about what's going on," she said.

"I have a terrible pain at the ball of my foot, and my marathon is on Sunday." My face felt hot. I knew I must not look like a marathoner. I was still ten pounds overweight from the pregnancy, and I didn't have the lean body or the stocky calf muscles more experienced runners developed through training, like I had years ago. My breasts were too large to fit into a sports bra, and the chafing of my thighs had left bloody rashes and scars.

She glanced down at my running shoes with the holes at the top near my toes. "Are these the shoes you run in?"

"Yes."

She tilted her head and drew one side of her mouth up. "Might be time for a new pair. I suggest swapping out every few months."

Extended leave from work had delivered a financial hit, so I'd had to be careful with spending these past few months. New running shoes would knock me back more than a hundred dollars. But there was no point telling her any of that, so I stared at my shoes and said, "Noted."

She dug her finger into the ball of my foot while making *hmm* noises. "Is this where it hurts?"

I flinched again, this time from the pain. "Yes."

"Does it feel like a golf ball is lodged in the ball of your foot?"

Was this a trick question? Perhaps golf-ball pain was a sign of something serious that would bench me from the race, like a stress fracture. I considered lying, but the truth boiled inside me like a poached egg until it leaked right out of my mouth.

"Yes, that's exactly what it feels like," I replied. My heart kicked up a few beats faster. I tucked my hands under my soft thighs, waiting for the verdict.

All of those months, when nothing had made sense to me but lacing up my sneakers, I'd turned to running to keep me alive. I'd run through the hot summer, into the fall. Day after day, my muscles had ached after torturing myself for hours on the trail. I'd needed to run, and now I needed her to say she could fix this.

"Good news. It's nerve pain, not a fracture. You can run as long as this pair of inserts helps your pain. Also, please do the usual icing and elevation." She peeled the adhesive off an insert and stuck it into my torn-up shoe.

"My foot won't snap in half if I run my marathon on Sunday?" I pressed.

"No, it won't. I hope the inserts help and you won't be in pain."

A simple fix. No MRIs, no physical therapy, no admonition to rest. I was so relieved that I wanted to cry. My heart swelled with purpose. *I can run. I can run!*

I smiled at the receptionist as I left.

The fall breeze tickled my salty neck outside the office building. I had already jammed the other insert into my sneaker, eager to give them a try. With my hands stuffed inside my jacket pockets, I passed by the animal rescue clinic where we'd adopted Ella. I was in such a good mood that I considered stopping in to buy her a special treat, but she already had plenty.

Around the corner, customers at the Australian-inspired café sipped their coffee, holding on to the last bit of sunny weather before the Northeast turned bitter cold by the end of the month. I still hadn't gotten coffee from there since my "allergic" reaction, whether real or not. As I rounded the corner from the café, an uncomfortable pulse rocketed through my arch. My foot was agitated even more from the inserts. *What a waste of money.* I'd been silly to believe my pain would disappear after walking with them, but it was still disappointing.

I took a deep breath before I entered our one-bedroom apartment. Truthfully, it wasn't easy coming home sometimes. It was a harsh reminder of the life that had been taken from us. No crying baby to nurture, no makeshift nursery in the den, and only the sound of our rescue lab whimpering at the door.

I sat on the entryway bench like a wilted flower. There I slipped off my sneakers, ripped out the inserts, and cried. Excited I was home, Ella darted up to me, and she pounded me with wet kisses when she realized I was upset.

"What's going on?" Gautam asked as he took off his headphones and got up from his makeshift office at the living room table. He walked over and sat next to me. I hid my face in my hands, thinking of how I'd fail to honor our daughter's memory.

"My foot still hurts," I stammered.

Gautam knelt to rub my foot. As he peeled off my sock, our dog gleefully licked my ankles. I was grateful for my pit crew. "Oh, no. How did the visit go?"

"The doctor cleared me and gave me inserts, but it didn't help like I expected," I said.

He sat next to me and put his arms around

me. "Maybe it was too much too soon," he said softly.

I shrugged off his hand. Grief had made me short-tempered. I wanted to be alone with my grief, on the pavement, running. I couldn't understand his hesitation. "You don't believe in me, do you?" I asked as I scanned his face.

"Why would you say that?" He asked looking surprised and hurt.

"Because you never did." I limped off into the bathroom, knowing that all I did was cause pain to those around me.

I turned on the sink and let the water turn hot on my hands. I longed to go for a run, to be alone on the trail. I wished those damn inserts had worked, but instead, I'd need to keep resting my foot. I knew family members would be relieved if I didn't run. They talked in hushed whispers as I pushed for more and more miles to distract me from the pain. The only freedom I had from grief was on the pavement, running.

I splashed the warm water on my face to soothe my blotchy skin from the tears. It scared me at times how running was the thing that grounded me on this planet. I knew I was being dramatic with the run-or-die nonsense that circled my thoughts, but it was true. Running was the only thing that gave me hope, and without the marathon . . . I might truly leave this world. The only thing that helped me quiet my mind was the sound of feet slapping against the pavement for hours along the river trail.

I grabbed a towel, opened the medicine cabinet, and pulled out the make-up remover. I washed the mascara streaks off my face and then went into the bedroom alone. On the bed, I pulled open my laptop, sank into bed, and propped myself up on the pillows. One pillow was streaked with make-up from when I had cried into it the other night. I opened a blank document and wrote to her, something I wished I had done more often.

Dear Laila:

It's November. It seems like just yesterday that it was cold March, moments after we left the hospital. We are coming up on eight months since we lost you. I don't understand how that's possible, eight months. If you were alive, I'd have that silly eight-month marker that I would pose you next to and make a post on social media about how you love giggling, nap time, and your daddy. Instead, I'm here without you, and my heart hurts.

I still have dreams about you. I don't think that'll ever stop, but this week, I had a dream I was looking at all of your pictures in a large pink binder, the kind that was my first photo album when I was a baby. It had fluffy pink fabric and lace. It's much different than only the three pictures I have of you tucked away in a small 4x6 flimsy photo album. That's how I realized it was a dream.

I think about you every day, and it brings me that warm, positive feeling, like when I'm holding you in my dreams. That feeling has become a part of me. I hope I feel it when I run the marathon. I hope that I'll have some type of message or sign from you when I'm running.

When I run, it brings me to this level of existence where I'm fighting, but when I get outside, it feels like my worries wash away, and I'm there, in that moment, doing the best I can. After enough miles, the runner's high takes over, and my body is ecstatic, feeling closer to you. Without running, it's been so hard. I don't know how I can make it through. I've been biking at the gym, and that's okay because I pray that I'll be on the start line soon.

Your little dog sister has been so good to us. She's hyper and crazy and keeps us on our feet, but I don't know how we would have healed without her presence taking over our apartment.

We still haven't moved out of our one-bedroom apartment yet. Moving almost feels like a betrayal because so much of your life was while I lived with your dad in this apartment. That's how I felt, too, when I switched my job. I spent so much time with you in my little, stuffy office at my old job that I felt bad leaving. But I did do the right thing.

My new job is challenging and has much longer hours and a commute, but I like the people around me. It helps that my coworkers are young and more focused on going out to bars than having kids. That makes a difference. I don't think I would do well if people talked about their kids all day, like at my last job.

Your dad's business is taking off. He has a couple more clients and is doing really well. He got his first close on a big deal last weekend, and I was so proud of him. He's working a lot of hours, though, and I feel guilty that he always needs to take care of me. We are hanging in there, my little love.

Gautam arrived back home and found me with Laila's memorial box. Even after eight months, I was embarrassed to have the box out around him. I wanted to protect him from the pain. When we first went through the items the hospital had carefully gathered for us, watching him cry had hurt so badly. But my therapist had suggested recently that it was best to go through the box together, as a couple. I needed to stop hiding my pain from him. I motioned him over, and he sat beside me. Ella jumped onto the bed and rested her head on my thigh.

"I'm sorry I was so upset earlier," I said.

His face softened. He stared down at the pink box, decorated with elephants, which held her pink knit hat, matching blanket, hospital brace-let, and photo album.

"I miss her, too," he said quietly.

My heart collapsed. I felt like an asshole for acting like grief only hurt me. I knew how hard it was for him, too.

"I know you do," I said, holding back more tears.

He kissed me on the cheek, and I hugged him.

"If you do the marathon, I promise I'll be there with Ella, cheering," he said. "We are on your side."

The morning before the marathon, I slept in. As I faded in and out of consciousness, I heard a voice reverberate against my ear drums. A man's voice. Angelic. Instead of feeling afraid, I didn't try to wake myself up. I took a leap of faith and let the voice guide me into sleep. The moment I did, it felt as though I were pulled forward, like I was riding a wooden rollercoaster.

As I roamed around an all-white room, the angelic presence towered over me. I felt the warmth awakening each cell in my body, fill-ing them with a frantic, elated motion. In my arms, Laila appeared, wrapped up in all white. My chest widened and grew like a hummingbird drunk with nectar. I clasped onto her for my life.

When I returned to consciousness, I woke up with something much greater than a good night's sleep. I wouldn't remember the dream until later in the day, and when I did, I almost curled into the ground and cried.

I took this as a sign that I would see Laila again during the race. I knew it.

CHAPTER NINETEEN

On the morning of the marathon, I stepped out of bed, careful not to wake Gautam. Since he wasn't a morning person, he'd meet me at the finish line. My family would meet me at mile twenty in Manayunk, near my sister's rowhome.

I held my breath; I could walk on my foot. No pain. I decided not to press my luck with my foot, so I hailed a cab for the one-mile trip to the start line. The driver dropped me off as close as he could with the road closures. As I walked down the parkway, I was grateful for my extra layers of puffy, cheap clothes from Goodwill.

Philadelphia was dark and quiet. I perched myself on the art museum steps and rubbed my foot as I watched the runners trickle in. A few runners posed at the top of the museum steps, making their best Rocky impression. To preserve my phone's battery, I didn't take it out. Instead, I watched the orange sunrise leak over the growing crowd of colorful runners.

Today is the day I'll see my daughter again.

I went down to the start line, and after shuffling through the thousands of runners, I glanced down at my phone. I had one percent battery life. Shit. It must not have charged last night. I was stuck with no way to contact my husband for a pep talk or in case something went wrong.

Maybe a miracle would happen, and suddenly my phone would come back to life. Instead, it died when the gun went off.

I knew from the runner who led my training group that I wasn't supposed to go out fast, but I did anyway. I blasted down the parkway and through the Italian Market in South Philly. I couldn't believe my foot didn't hurt, but by mile nine, my belly was twisted in horrific knots. I buckled over. My cramps grew worse than my contractions had been. I managed to run-walk as runners whizzed by me. Then I saw the woman I had done the twenty-mile training run with; her ponytail swayed rhythmically to her pace. I wanted to run with her, but after she passed me, she disappeared into the distance.

A runner next to me clutched his calf and yelled from the pain. We hobbled together but didn't speak. I could hear the techno buzz coming from his headphones. I was so slow that even the costumed runners caught up to us: a monkey and a banana. I wanted to give up.

At mile twenty, I saw my dad in Manayunk. Just like during races in college, he had found me on the trail to surprise me and cheer me on. I told him my stomach was giving out, and he laughed and encouraged me. As he jogged along the sidewalk with me, I saw my mom and sister, who handed me some goldfish. I forgot to tell them to message my husband and let him know that I'd be at the finish line in a few miles.

In those final miles, no miraculous sign fell from the sky like I had dreamed of during those months of training. My daughter didn't magically appear in the air, unloading my burden of grief by proving somewhere else, like heaven, existed. I wouldn't get to hold her in my arms again. I was too out of breath to cry, but I did anyway. I was desperate to call my husband and hear his voice, to tell him how wrong I'd been—a marathon was too much too soon. All of those miles away from him hadn't fixed my grief.

My breathing turned shallow. A man dressed as Forrest Gump passed me. I could see the calf-cramp man on Kelly Drive. The costumed monkey runner re-appeared and shuffled down the road; I wondered if the banana had dropped out.

Most of the crowd of cheering spectators was gone by now. I heard a few slow claps as I neared the finish line, and finally, I could see my husband in his heavy winter coat. He was there. He had found me. I saw Ella, too, a black figure in the distance, wiggling with excitement.

I picked up the pace, and after I crossed the finish line, I collapsed into his warm arms. Ella joined in the hug, leaping onto us.

"I tried to call you. It's been almost six hours," Gautam said, his voice sounding coarse. He was worried. I realized that he didn't want anything to happen to me. We only had each other now to survive and to remember our daughter. We had a responsibility to make our love last a lifetime. He was the only person who loved her as much as I did.

"I'm slow, remember?" I reminded him. "You didn't need to worry."

CHAPTER TWENTY

I finally hallucinated my daughter. The vision didn't come from my first or second marathon. The apparition arrived a year and a half after my loss, while working at a bereavement retreat for loss moms. At the suggestion of a loss mom in my support group, I watched the movie *Return to Zero* with Gautam. Together, we watched the story of a couple whose son had died, and Gautam didn't budge. "You should go to this retreat," he said. "They understand."

I did. I enrolled in the program and went to the retreat in Colorado Springs. A local loss mom picked up a few of us at the airport and drove us two hours to the Rocky Mountains. I had hiked the Manitou Incline, I had met women in the same pain, and I had changed. I had been asked to come back by the nonprofit leader the following fall, this time as a workshop facilitator to help work the retreat.

This was a surprise to me. I had never considered myself a role-model griever, but I seemed to have made an impression.

This year, the retreat took place in a spiritual

center in Phoenicia, New York. I had learned through the program that there are spiritual centers all over the states, often blessed by shamans, loaded with crystal rocks, and surrounded by nature. This one, in particular, is supposed to have a "sacred being" who looks over the property. The original owner supposedly channeled and wrote down its messages near the revered pond.

I had to take the train to New York City and then a connecter to Hudson. I loved spending the day on an Amtrak. To help pass the time, I graded a stack of college essays. I was teaching an English class part-time at college as part of my master's program.

The other co-facilitator, Betsy from Washington, picked me up from the station in her rental SUV. We drove down the winding roads and over the Rip Van Winkle Bridge, heading into the Catskills.

"Was Rip Van Wrinkle a real person?" Betsy asked as the roads turned remote and woodsy. The sky was getting dark.

I paused and reached for my phone. "I think he's make-believe," I said as I refreshed my memory about "Rip Van Wrinkle," a story by Washington Irving about a man who fell asleep near the Catskills and awoke decades later. It reminded me of grief. It had already been over a year since Laila had passed, and I felt like I'd been asleep the entire time and that the reality I was living in was distorted.

"Strange to name a bridge after someone

imaginary," she added as she shook her head. She kept her eyes glued to the road. The winding roads were sharp, and it looked like a deer could jump out at any moment. "I'm glad you're here with me, this center is really in the middle of nowhere."

I agreed.

We made it to the wellness center. By the time we arrived, the surrounding area was covered in thick darkness, the kind that's only found in a small town far from any city, deep in the woods.

We found the parking lot to the main center and walked into the lobby. At the front desk, a twenty-something-year-old was sipping a cup of tea. He looked like someone I would have known at my liberal arts college from an animal rights group or met later at a yoga class. Crystal rocks were for sale on the desk corner, and mandala beads hung from the jewelry display. Betsy and I signed our names on the guest list, and she gave him the nonprofit's credit card.

"Welcome to Menla," he said as he brought his hands together as though in prayer. He gave us a quick tour of the main building, which included a small gift shop and common area. The cafeteria still had warm vegetarian food set out. My stomach rumbled at the sight, needing more than coffee and the snacks I had on the train.

He looked at us, sensing our fatigue. "Why don't you eat before the kitchen closes? I can do the rest of the tour tomorrow. It's too dark now to show you the rest of the property."

"That works," Betsy said, and then we

grabbed plates and headed to the buffet.

The squash soup was cold, and there was no butter for my multigrain bread. *Better than nothing*. At the table, as Betsy went over the logistics, her feathered earrings danced around her cheeks.

"We both have one cabin to be in charge of when the guests arrive tomorrow. I have the moms with living children, and you'll have the cabin for the moms with no living children. Does that work?"

"That works for me," I said. Betsy was incredibly mindful about making sure everyone felt comfortable, those with living kids and those without. Although we had all gone through loss, there was a difference for moms without living kids. You never know what might trigger someone. On bad days, I would struggle to hear about someone's daughter.

I liked being in charge of my own cabin and making it a safe place.

Of course, we had forgotten to bring flashlights. Before we left, the front desk clerk let us borrow lamp-like flashlights. My cabin looked ominous in the dark. Betsy left her headlights on so I could set up each room with the gift baskets she handed me from her trunk. I double-fluffed the pillows, straightened the clean blankets, and made the rooms look as welcoming as possible, as it had been for me when I had been a retreat participant. Then she drove me across the property to her cabin, and I stayed in one of the extra rooms. We didn't want to sleep alone.

One night, I was leading the group mediation in the yoga studio. This studio was unlike any I had seen before, certainly not like the ones in the city. This oval room had floor-to-ceiling glass windows with a view of the surrounding woods.

I stood with my hands interlocked with other loss moms. In only a few days, we had become a sisterhood of our own. Teacup candles burned in a circle, one for each lost baby, and sage burned for us. The melody of wind chimes and sound bowls reverberated throughout the studio. While the other women had their eyes closed, whispering words like *ohm*, I cracked one open.

Then I saw Laila. All of those years, in my first marathon and then my second, I had searched for her but with no luck. Now she was here with me.

She was a toddler, the age she would be if she hadn't died, and holding hands with Betsy. She was wearing a pink dress, high frilly socks, and white sneakers. A gold bracelet was around her wrist. *Come to me*, I mouthed to her. *Come here, baby*. I motioned for her to come to my side. She had thick black hair in a short bob and bangs that fell over her large, wide brown eyes. As the candle in the center of the circle flickered and danced, Laila smiled and waddled to my side. I stared down, and she clasped my hand.

When the lights came back on, she vanished. I excused myself and went to the restroom. I let out a quick cry in the stall and then went to the sink and splashed cold water on my face. I didn't want the other women to see me crying. As a workshop leader, I wanted to remain steady for their grief, not my own.

Back in the cabin, I called my husband on the landline, since the service wasn't good with cellphones.

"I saw her," I told him.

"What did she look like?" he asked.

It warmed my heart that he took these sightings seriously and wanted to know each detail. I described exactly what I had seen.

"I miss you," he said.

"I'll be home soon."

When I left those woods, it was raining. Betsy drove past Woodstock, and we stopped at a boutique chocolate store in Hudson near my train. The shop had vintage candy jars, fudge, and an espresso bar. I only ordered a coffee to use the restroom as a courtesy, and let the cold water run hot on my hands to warm up. Afterward, Betsy dropped me off and I took shelter from the rain in the dark coral train station. On the long train ride that went through the Hudson Valley, I felt like a different person. I was a little lighter, a little freer. Somehow, I knew, she did exist, only not in the same way as us. She was here with us. She'd never left. She was telling us in her own way.

After a few years, Ernie the plant was barely alive. His once brown branches were pale yellow, and most of his leaves were dead. We had to save him, and luckily hardware stores remained open during the onset of the global pandemic. In a last-ditch effort to revive Ernie, we set out to the local

hardware store in our masks and gloves and purchased some plant food. I clipped the leaves, and
Gautam removed a dead branch with attentive-
ness like a surgeon. We replaced the bulb for his
plant light. We couldn't let Ernie die.

Weeks later, Gautam noticed a small burst
of green by the roots. Over time, that little green
sprout grew. "Ernie had a baby," we joked to each
other as we watched life before us when the world
was shutting down. We named Ernie's offspring
"baby sprout." Ernie was so close to death, but
now this miracle was right in front of our faces. I
rubbed my fingers in his soil and gingerly touched
baby sprout; I touched my own belly with wonder.
So close to death, but now there's life.

Acknowledgments

I wrote this story during my M.F.A. program at Drexel University. Nomi Eve, this memoir wouldn't have been possible without your guidance. You encouraged me to work on my memoir as part of the brand-new writing program at Drexel. Thank you for admitting me into the first cohort of writers. You changed my life.

I would also like to extend my gratitude towards the faculty members at Drexel University who provided mentorship on this memoir: Kathryn Craft, Ann Garvin, Erin Celello, Alexia Arthurs, Julie Cantrell, and Katie Rose Guest Pryal. Thank you for your encouragement from other faculty members, Elizabeth Kimball, Maegan Poland, Harriet Milan, Janet Benton, Scott Stein, my classmates, and my students at Drexel.

Before my M.F.A. program, I spent a few summers at the Southampton Writers Conference. Special thanks to my teachers and mentors, Matt Klam, Paul Harding, and Melissa Bank. Roger Rosenblatt, thank you for your support with this story.

Thank you to the other fabulous writing conferences I've attended, Tin House (Lance and India), for the exceptional writer's workshop and Tom Jenks at *Narrative Magazine* for your support early on with my memoir writing.

I sincerely appreciate the literary magazines that published or supported my work. Thank you, Southampton Review, *Barren Magazine*, and *Macro Magazine*, for your support with this manuscript.

Thank you to my publisher, Alexa Bigwarfe and Kat Biggie Press; I'm so grateful for your commitment to publishing stories like mine to help bereaved parents. To my designer Michelle Fairbanks for bringing my vision for the book cover to life, and Cayce LaCorte for your help and flawless execution of this project.

Thank you to my editor, Jefferson, for your kind words and attention to detail.

Without my early readers, I'm not sure how I would have known if I was going in the right direction. Thank you for giving me the momentum and encouragement to keep writing: Mario Giannini, Rebecca Salowe, Dan Driscoll, Daniel Horn, and Rebecca Ingalls.

To my friends who were there for me after Laila left our world; Tatianna, Zoe, Emi, and others. To my manager, Rachel Tsiouris-Gabriele, thank you for showing compassion and helping me support my dreams to write this story while working.

The phenomenal medical staff helped me birth Laila, and my second daughter, Ashanti. Dr.

C. the world is simply a better place with you in it. Thank you for taking care of my family.

My Return to Zero: H.O.P.E. warriors, Kiley and Betsy. Thank you for making the world for bereaved parents less lonely. To other wonderful organizations, such as UNITE Grief. Ann Coyle, thank you.

I've had the pleasure of meeting many brave parents who lost their children, and I think of your babies often. Most of your babies' names are on the cover page, because so much of my story is all of our stories. For the children I haven't met yet, but I know I will get the honor of hearing your story from this book, I love you and your brave parents already.

I sincerely appreciate the love of my family, friends, and mentors. To the Bazaz family. To my sister-in-law, Komal, thank you for your love of reading and for being there for me. To my parents, you always came over to visit me on my hard days. My sister, Lara, and brother, Christian.

To my great-grandmother, Hilda, and my grandmother, Vicki. To my great-aunt, Diane.

My husband, thank you for being by my side and letting me write about such a personal moment in our lives. To our silly dog, Ella, whose unconditional love helped save us. To my newborn daughter, Ashanti, who took many naps on my chest while I wrote and revised this manuscript.

To my first daughter, Laila. Thank you for making me a mother.

ABOUT THE AUTHOR

Photo by Christian Hunold

Leah Mele-Bazaz is a wife and mother. She graduated from Drexel University with an M.F.A in
Creative Writing, where she also works as an
English adjunct faculty member. In 2020, her
memoir about Laila was nominated as a finalist for
the *Southampton Review Nonfiction Prize*, and
subsequently, portions of her memoir appeared
in *Barren Magazine* and *Macro Magazine*, and
she won *Barren Magazine*'s December Instagram
Poetry Contest. She also has presented her
research on pregnancy loss at academic conferences and has volunteered at the nonprofit Return
to Zero: H.O.P.E.

When Leah gave birth to her stillborn daughter, Laila, she didn't know how to handle this
type of grief. She went through depression and

isolation, and she had trouble finding ways to show she was still a mother. She started writing this story days after she came home from the hospital without her baby and kept a daily journal documenting her grief. With encouragement from her writing mentor, she applied to graduate school, turning her observations and experiences into a manuscript. During her last semester at school, she finished this book and gave birth to her second daughter, Ashanti.

When Leah isn't waking up at dawn to write before work, she loves running in Philadelphia and cozying up with a new book. You can visit her at leahmelebazaz.com.